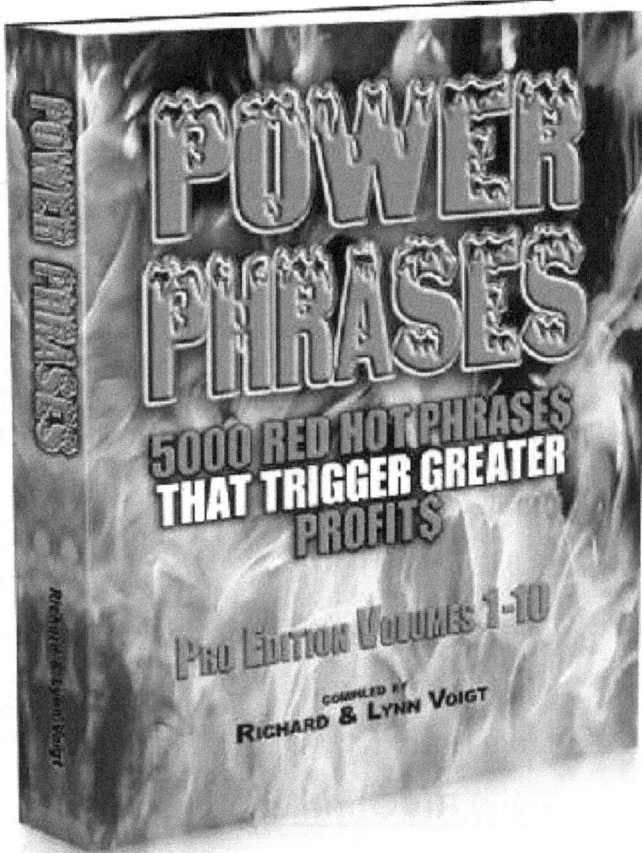

POWER PHRASES – Pro Edition (Complete Series)
5000 Power Phrases That Trigger Greater Profits

© 2013 by RIVO Inc – All Rights Reserved!

ISBN-13: 978-1-940961-11-8
ISBN-10: 1940961114

First Printing, 2013

Printed in the United States of America

To Access More Powerful Marketing Tools Visit:

www.RIVObooks.com

www.RIVOinc.com

www.WisconsinGarden.com

POWER PHRASES

Pro Edition Complete Series Volumes 1-10

5000 POWER PHRASES THAT TRIGGER GREATER PROFITS

-·|·-•·*'''''*·•·_·|·_•**•-·|·-•·*'''''*·•-·|·-

Compiled by

Richard & Lynn Voigt
I.M. Education Specialists

Introduction: Pro Edition 5000 Power Phrases

Powerful Phrases, Headlines, Sub Headlines, Slogans, Bullet Points and Interview Sound Bites are perhaps the most powerful marketing tools mankind has ever created. They are the lifeblood behind every business venture are the ultimate secret weapon of Millionaire Marketers.

No matter whether you are introducing or promoting a brand new product, teaching a "How To" skill, building a website, or simply sending an email, using the perfect power phrase is crucial to capturing and holding eyeballs and producing greater marketing profits.

In today's world every word you use has measurable impact. Each word can produce emotional psychological buttons that trigger psychological reactions. Successful advertisers understand that using an effective power phrase is a true art form that turns "wants" into instant gratification "needs." Once artfully triggered, any niche market can instantly create more protifable conversions.

Now it's your turn to personalize this incredible collection of 5000 Power Phrases in ways that instantly advance your own effective marketing skills as you create new and power phrases, slogans, presentations, bullet points, or interview sound bites that take you to the next level.

Whether starting or running a small business, writing an ad, coming up with a memorable slogan, making a major corporate presentation, bullet points, creating a video, writing a book, searching for the perfect slogan, teaching a lesson or book report, your creative use of these Power Phrases can capture more eyeballs and produce some amazing rewards quickly turning you into a Marketing Genius. Now, it's your turn to make the magic happen!

POWERFUL POWER WORDS

Never underestimate the role Power Words play in your sales headlines, sub headlines, presentations, and skilled copywriting tasks. Ever word matters because we are wired to react to words that inspire us to take action.

Specific Power Words paint pictures and create images of positive emotional values in the mind of how we want things to be, enticing the mind for finding solutions that ease pain and prime and pump desires. Using words like easy, new, quick, exciting, convenient, and improve draw readers into taking a desired winning action.

Here are 500 Power Words you should consider using in future marketing campaigns to help paint pictures, sell ideas, and market your message effectively.

1	Inventive		21	Hot-Off-The-Press
2	Booming		22	Discovery
3	Victorious		23	Call-To-Action
4	Blast		24	Money-Shot
5	To-The-Next-Level		25	Evasive
6	Buy-Now		26	Commando
7	Fool-Proof		27	Unexpected
8	Allegedly		28	Magical-Formula
9	Cement-The-Relationship		29	Nothing-To-Lose
10	Wealthy		30	Swan-Song
11	Dependable		31	World-Stage
12	Limited-Supply		32	Crunch-Time
13	Agent-For-Change		33	Future
14	Inching		34	Blunder
15	Numb		35	Bad-Ass
16	Uncover		36	Negligent
17	Private		37	Drilled-Down
18	You-Snooze-You-Lose		38	Bust
19	Threatened		39	Adventure
20	Grinding-Halt		40	Off-The-Hook

41	God-Forsaken	81	Solution
42	Daring	82	Think-Free
43	Fantasy	83	Pissed-Off
44	Independent	84	Seriousness
45	Automated	85	Over-Saturated
46	Amateur	86	The-Big-Boys
47	Exotic	87	Products
48	Reliable	88	Genius
49	Grind	89	Pounce
50	Enhance-Enhanced	90	Create-Creative
51	Eager-Anticipation	91	Pandora's-Box
52	Beauty-Beautiful	92	Rising-Through-The-Ranks
53	Bruised-Ego	93	Soaking-Wet
54	Zen-Master	94	Hysterical
55	Ads	95	Make-It-Easy
56	Limited	96	Clear-Cut
57	Reckless	97	Strong-stronger
58	Rumor	98	Impossible-Situation
59	Gut-Wrenching-Agony	99	Emulate
60	On-The-Line	100	Unleash-Unleashed
61	Accept-Acceptance	101	Update
62	Subject-Lines	102	Bonanza
63	Intense	103	Classic-Classical
64	Eagerly	104	Demand-Demanding
65	Intimidation	105	Life-Threatening
66	Sleeping-Like-A-Log	106	Empowered
67	Live-The-Lifestyle	107	Quality
68	Work-For-Yourself	108	Winning-Attitude
69	Oozing	109	Timed-Offer
70	Lambaste	110	Valuable
71	Marketing-Campaigns	111	Astonish-Astonishing
72	Headlines	112	Endured
73	Eureka-Moment	113	Confident-Confidence
74	Intrinsic	114	Bad-Hair-Day
75	Butt-Ugly	115	Facts-Speak-For-Themselves
76	Manhandled		
77	Bank-Account	116	Laser-Like-Focus
78	Sucker-Punched	117	Self-Publish
79	Professional	118	Relevant
80	Enabled	119	Escape
		120	Oblivious

121	Stuttering	161	Caught-In-The-Act
122	Hassle-Free	162	Neurotic
123	Timed-To-Perfection	163	Sidelined
124	Impressive	164	Materialize
125	Pre-Occupied	165	Entrepreneurial-Spirit
126	Fashionable	166	Never-Seen-Before
127	Cold-Hard-Facts	167	Killer
128	Scoff	168	Genie-In-The-Bottle
129	Inspire-Inspiration	169	Ornate
130	Explosive	170	Everyone-And-His-Dog
131	Easy-Easily	171	Lethal-Weapon
132	Year-After-Year	172	Important
133	Loophole	173	Behind-Closed-Doors
134	Toolbox	174	Slay
135	Enraged	175	Humbling-Experience
136	Platinum	176	Out-There
137	Secret	177	Ridicule
138	While-Supplies-Last	178	Health-Healthy
139	Achieve-Achievement	179	Lopsided
140	No-Nonsense	180	Hot-To-Trot
141	Luxury	181	Priceless
142	Quick-Quickly	182	Save
143	Affection	183	Knowledge
144	Mercilessly	184	Money
145	Nano-Second	185	Bragging-Rights
146	Critical	186	Common-Sense
147	Guru	187	Petrified
148	Money-Back-Guarantee	188	Benefits
149	Ego-Egotistical	189	Bulletproof
150	Feel-Their-Pain	190	Unique
151	Bandit	191	Demand
152	Budget	192	Save-Money
153	Arrogant	193	Gnarled
154	Fortunes	194	Day-Job-Blues
155	Sweet	195	Wrath
156	Unfazed	196	Drama
157	Snuggled	197	Cure
158	Shrinks	198	Proven
159	Wise-Decision	199	Relished
160	Yearning	200	Missing-Link

8

201	Security	241	Overcome
202	Services	242	Freedom
203	Bled-Dry	243	Pulling-My-Leg
204	Work-Less	244	Dogged-Determination
205	Boredom	245	Inflame
206	Obsolete	246	Prestige
207	Shocked-Shocking	247	Irrefutable-Evidence
208	Maximize	248	Duped
209	Relax	249	Propel
210	Cutting-Edge	250	Threatening
211	Lure	251	Zero-Credibility
212	Limited-Time-Offer	252	Handicap
213	Austere	253	High-Value
214	Military-Precision	254	Power-Powerful
215	Safe-Safety-Safely	255	Experience
216	Popular	256	Blink-Of-An-Eye
217	Required	257	Scientifically-Proven
218	Sought-After	258	Revealed
219	Strong-As-Steel	259	Ensure
220	Sneak-Peak	260	Brake-Down
221	On-The-Money	261	Soothing
222	Plan-Planning	262	Emotions-Emotional
223	Devastating	263	Now
224	Free	264	Convenient
225	X-ray-Vision	265	Down-To-The-Wire
226	Crack-The-Code	266	Be-Your-Own-Boss
227	Customer-Service	267	Instant-Instantly
228	Slaughter	268	Pimped-Out
229	Worry	269	Acclaim
230	Exciting	270	Advertise-Advertising
231	Discount	271	Advance-Advancement
232	Comfort-Comfortable	272	Endless
233	Millimeter-Perfection	273	Insane
234	Foaming	274	Accomplish-Accomplishment
235	Mutation		
236	Lazily	275	Options
237	Brilliant-Brilliance	276	Pathetic
238	Counter-Intuitive	277	Mastermind
239	You	278	Live-Longer
240	Trial-Run	279	Bailed-Out
		280	Fumigate

281	Stress-Free	321	You-Your
282	Transfer	322	Hands-On
283	Languid	323	Broken
284	Rhythmic	324	Secure
285	Energy-Energetic	325	Survey
286	Stockpiled	326	Mistrusted
287	Top-Notch	327	Fun
288	Jail-Break	328	Rookie
289	Viral	329	Shear-Dread
290	Mastery	330	Breaking-Out-In-Cold-Sweat
291	Little-Known	331	Desire-Desires-Desirable
292	Strength	332	Best
293	Sale-Sales	333	Savvy
294	Love	334	Secret-Sauce
295	Nuance	335	Challenge-Challenging
296	Valued-Customer	336	Iron-Clad
297	Throw-Away	337	Self-Determined
298	Simple-Fix	338	Pleasure-Pleasurable
299	Life-Changing	339	Bend-Over-Backwards
300	Battle-Hardened	340	Eliminate
301	Words-That-Sell	341	Fail-Failure
302	Wrangle	342	Attract-Attraction
303	Top	343	Tailored
304	Disaster	344	Sabotaged
305	Mindset	345	Customer-Acquisition
306	Pirated	346	Freak-Out
307	Drenched	347	Awesome
308	Tingling-Sensation	348	Autopsy
309	How-To	349	Ecstatic
310	Secrets	350	Successful
311	Ripped-Off	351	Memories
312	Reputation	352	Aches-And-Pains
313	Guarantee-Guaranteed	353	Insider-Information
314	Express	354	Deal-Of-The-Day
315	Monster-Deal	355	Results
316	Face-The-Facts	356	From-Scratch
317	Win-Win	357	Flawed
318	Knowing-The-Ropes	358	Winning
319	Prize-Money	359	Reality
320	Butterfly-Effect	360	Disgruntled

361	Scour	401	Gratifying
362	Mysterious	402	Disappear-Disappearing
363	Pain-Free	403	Personalized
364	Hardcore	404	Distinguishing-Features
365	Ambition	405	Save-Time
366	Financially-Ruined	406	Stacked-In-Your-Favor
367	In-A-Blink	407	Implodes
368	Time-Saver	408	Come-Clean
369	Personality	409	Ninja-Master
370	Clearance	410	Confidential
371	Passion	411	Wealth-Mentality
372	Teased	412	Having-The-Edge
373	Attitude	413	Supercharged
374	Bulldog-Determination	414	Self-Employed
375	Zero-Risk	415	Surprise
376	Unlock	416	Excuses
377	Cool-As-Ice	417	Humiliated
378	Deadline	418	Hotshot
379	Snail-Mail	419	Brand-Brandable
380	Deluxe	420	Deadly-Rage
381	Profit-Profitable	421	Business-Plan
382	Blood-Thirsty	422	Research
383	Just-Plain-Wrong	423	Jumpstart
384	Proven-Over-Time	424	Decision
385	Life-And-Death	425	Satisfaction
386	Empathy	426	Homemade
387	Gain	427	Test-Drive
388	Fair-Share	428	Unrelenting
389	Rare	429	Defies-Gravity
390	Leader-Leadership	430	Voodoo
391	List	431	Shambles
392	Alarm-Alarming	432	Feelings
393	Prospect	433	Sales-Copy
394	Fatal	434	Story-Telling
395	Vigor	435	Plain-Free
396	Obstacles	436	Sweeten-The-Deal
397	Yes	437	Dirty-Tricks
398	Outsider	438	Afford-Affordable
399	Determined	439	Absolute-Absolutely
400	New	440	Improve-Improved

441	Better	471	Belittled-Belittling
442	Make-Money	472	Spartan
443	All-Natural	473	Copywriting
444	Self-Sufficient	474	Step-By-Step
445	More	475	Transformative
446	Willingly	476	Too-Good-To-Be-True
447	Sweet-Spot	477	Download
448	Dream-Come-True	478	Rake-In
449	30-Day-Guarantee	479	Brand-New
450	Shame	480	Dominate-Domination
451	Shrewdness	481	Trapped
452	Personal-Story	482	Original
453	Compact	483	Author-Authority
454	Heavenly	484	Disarmed-Disarming
455	Door-Buster	485	Intuitive
456	Word-Of-Mouth	486	Open-Minded
457	Pillaged	487	Admire-Admired
458	Personally	488	Total-Fluke
459	Under-Siege	489	Fear-Factor
460	Email	490	Lukewarm
461	Distinguished	491	Carelessness
462	Voice-Your-Opinion	492	Moolah
463	Blew-My-Mind	493	Scratching-The-Surface
464	Compel-Compelling	494	Bribe-Bribed
465	Resourceful	495	Uncanny
466	Brutal-Truth	496	Connected
467	Order--Now	497	Self-Respect
468	Decision-Making	498	Web-Of-Intrigue
469	Blown-Away	499	Bottom-Line
470	Protect	500	Efficient

POWER PHRASES

Pro Edition Volumes 1-10 – 0001 - 5000

5000 Power Phrases That Trigger Greater Profits

Begin Selecting & Customizing Your Perfect Marketing Phrase

1	Negative Advertising Effect
2	Your Future Just Got Closer
3	Activate Your Risk Free Trial Right This Second
4	Know You Can Win This War
5	Why I'll Never Look Back
6	Why Your Focus May Need To Shift To Compete Online
7	Would You Consider Lower Payments
8	What's Your Screen Presence
9	Setting The Stage For Education
10	You Won't Like This
11	No One Really Likes Long Canned Messages
12	The Right Now Sale
13	Are They Looking For Reasons To Delete
14	Things That Kill Business
15	It's Amazing How Well This Works
16	The Real Secrets
17	Ever Wonder What You're Doing Wrong
18	For The Woman Who Needlessly Is Older Than She Looks
19	This Isn't Common Wisdom
20	Your New Account Balance
21	Look What Our Customers Are Saying

60	Avoiding These Unpleasant Experiences Was My Selfish Dream Until Now
61	Listen To The Voice Within
62	When Piracy Increases Sales
63	Writing Headlines That Hook Your Reader
64	Ditch Unflattering Clothes
65	You Don't Have To Be Brilliant
66	Harness The Power Of The Internet
67	Way More Is Possible
68	Deviation From Failure
69	Try Lots And Lots Of Stuff
70	Aren't You Fed Up Yet
71	Frame Of Reference
72	The Price Is Rising Rising Rising
73	No One Is Left Behind
74	Still Cutting Corners On Sleep
75	Fantastic Home Business For Your Entire Family
76	Post Your Ad For Free
77	Play Them Back Anywhere
78	Global Speaking Engagements
79	Your Business And Reputation Is At Stake
80	Feeling OK At Being Rich
81	Tenacious Misconceptions
82	Deliver Formidable Products As Easy As Turning On The Faucet
83	Either You Want To Succeed Or You Don't
84	You'll Want Me Around
85	Create Your Own Video Syndication
86	Rewards Are Two-Fold
87	Create A How To System
88	Is There Enough Value
89	Transforming Negative Energy Into Inspiration
90	Set It Up In 30-Seconds
91	Marketers Need To Relax Their Mind
92	It Could Cause Panic In The Streets
93	Take Advantage Of Our Knowledge
94	A Very Profitable Offer
95	Urge Quick Action
96	I Personally Recommend This Because

211	I've Already Added Tons Of Bonuses
212	Turn Your Sub Headlines Into Questions
213	People Are Not Readers So Infotain Them
214	Advertising Now Free And Viral
215	Scratch Everything
216	Will Your Traffic Be There Tomorrow
217	Duel Readership Paths
218	Helping You To Shake Off Anymore Failures
219	Don't Cry To Me If You Miss This One
220	Are You Overrating Your Talents
221	Create A Marketing Fire Online
222	Perfect For Newbies
223	Let Them Make The Sale
224	Hi And Hello
225	Inventive Value Added Provider
226	Tell It Like Your Life Depends Upon It
227	When They See Themselves They Buy
228	Trading Hours Hard Work And Skill For Dollars
229	If You're Not Online You're Screwed
230	Make It Available In All Formats
231	Domain Alarm
232	Sell It As A Product
233	Why Failure Is Important
234	Tried It All And Nothing Still Works
235	Have Someone Interview You
236	Ponder While You Poop
237	Runs On Minimal Input
238	Put Thos Old Tactics To Bed Now
239	Try Something Different
240	Wanted To Get Back To You Quickly
241	To Sue Or Not To Sue
242	Show Up And The Rest Is History
243	Click Here To Activate
244	Giving You The Finest Quality
245	More Than Just Grabbing Their Attention
246	Is This Counter Productive
247	Turn Scanners Into A Readers
248	Avoid Criticism

19

325	Most Definitely It Is The Real Deal
326	Need To Drill Down Even Farther
327	Enter This Code And Save Money
328	Enjoy It Anywhere
329	Save This For Later
330	Just What We've Been Praying For
331	Slick Design
332	Why Fail Like 98% Of Marketers
333	Cash Siphoning Secrets You Were Never Meant To See
334	Charge A Thousand Times More Money
335	Another Major Player Arrived
336	How To Automate Your Marketing
337	Creating New Value
338	Bombarded With Fake Proof And Screenshots
339	Powerhouse Advertising And Profit Sharing
340	Changing At Break Neck Speed
341	You Can Never Have Enough Customers
342	Choosing The Perfect Product
343	Act Now
344	Deliver The Best You Can
345	From Trash To Cash
346	Mobile Experiential Marketing
347	Use Pressure To Prevent Procrastination
348	Find Your Sweet Spot
349	Feelings Reflect Body Posture Thoughts And Words You Use
350	A Lifetime Of Success
351	Referral Promotions
352	For Those On The Move
353	I Must Admit At First I Was Skeptical
354	No Gimmicks No Gadgets Just Hits
355	I'll See You On The Other Side Of The Mouse
356	Success Needs You
357	An Impromptu Workshop
358	Don't Do This Too Quickly
359	Yes These Videos Are Cool
360	Use The First One Soon
361	Years Of Experience
362	Almost Quit Twice

401	Free Access Link
402	Don't Keep Making The Same Mistakes
403	Never Be Stuck For Words Again
404	Need A Coat Of Fresh Paint
405	Earners Unite And Grow Together Earn Together
406	Instantly Unlock This Highly Sensitive And Confidential Information
407	Let's Begin Our Venture
408	Look At You
409	Activate Your Free Account Now
410	What Are We In For
411	Improve Your Life
412	Techno Junkie Discovers eGold Mine
413	Where Can You Enjoy This
414	My 2 Hour Work Day
415	One Little Button With Big Results
416	It's Woven Into The Entire Process
417	Feeding On Someone Else's Success
418	Qualities Of A Wealthy Person
419	Communicate It So Simply That They Get It Immediately
420	Is It Appropriate To Dress Conservatively
421	Well Enough Is Enough
422	Who's Your Sponsor
423	Isn't Financial Slavery A Bummer
424	Lure vs. Lull
425	You Truly Deserve The Best
426	With A Solid Foundation Growth Is Exciting
427	Not To Be Continued
428	Never Before Release
429	Profit Plugging Reports
430	Tired Of Worrying About Your Job And Money
431	Tired Of All The Hype
432	The Question I Always Hear
433	Losing vs. Keeping
434	Protect Your Ideas
435	Implications And Actions
436	Soften Your Knees When Standing
437	Rarely Used Ways To Upgrade Your Ad
438	What If People Don't Buy

24

514	Ask Them For Recommendations
515	Owning The First Google Page - Priceless
516	Kickin' Butt & Takin' Names
517	Who Says You're Wasting Your Time
518	Let It Shine
519	Wisdom Based Upon Damn Good Advice
520	People Find Time For Things They Care About
521	Become A Unique Specimen
522	Legitimate Online Money Making
523	Coaching Session With Me
524	Shatter The Traffic Myth
525	As In Totally Free
526	Accelerated Business Growth
527	Did You Enjoy It
528	Your Most Powerful Resource
529	Repetition Has Proven To Increase Sales
530	Instant Access To The Gold Standard Of Internet Marketing
531	Collect Valuable Things
532	Don't Do What Everyone Else Is Doing
533	9 Billion Websites Equals - Unlimited Customers
534	Ensure SEO Success
535	Bonus Comprehensive Videos
536	Marketing Socionomics
537	Fun Powerful Word Exercises
538	Had Enough Technology Lately
539	Power Of Emotions With Technology
540	Many Ask To Come Aboard But Few Are Chosen
541	View Based Conversation
542	Wrecking Ball Destroying Your Financial Opportunities
543	Send Me Your New Report
544	Why These Are Terminal
545	Unzip Your Future
546	They Chose To Join
547	Your New 2-1/2 Hour Work Day
548	Working Hard Without Reward
549	Take Notes Of What You Say On Video
550	Hiding Under A Rock
551	Give Me Some Money Making Ideas

552	Put All Of Your Marketing On Autopilot
553	Million Dollar Program Isn't A Fluke
554	Chance To Change Everything
555	A Virtual Circle Of Growth
556	Readers Not Browsers
557	Mastering Headlines
558	Sharing Your Story Of Struggle
559	Open Your Traffic Treasure Chest
560	Start Recording Face-To-Face Videos
561	Web Poll Survey
562	You Need Them - They Don't Need You
563	What Do You Need To Clean Up
564	I Hope This Doesn't Freak You Out
565	Takes You Well Beyond The Basics
566	Want Big Paydays Virtually Overnight
567	It Was At The Moment I Gave Up
568	Expertise Comes From Experience
569	Partnership Assistance
570	Thanks In Advance
571	Simple Questions That Evoke Massive Response
572	Can We Do This Together
573	Get Your Arms Around This
574	Destroy The Competition Literally Overnight
575	Black Weekend Blowout
576	Effective Social Bookmarking Strategies
577	Private Video Bonus
578	You May Only Be Missing This One Thing
579	Rustle Up Some Marketing Muscle
580	Low Fat Marketing
581	Build Income First Then Build Your Business
582	The Best One Dollar You Ever Spent
583	Even My Wife Enjoys Doing This
584	How Do You Become A Whale Marketer
585	Feel The Power Of Your List In Action
586	I'm No Mother Teresa
587	A Well Deserved Victory
588	Don't Listen To The Parrot Heads
589	Stand With Shoulders Back

590	Wealth Revealed
591	Cutting Edge Resources Where Prospects Contact YOU
592	Increase Traffic Conversions By 500% Or More With Splash Pages
593	So Why Share Great Ideas
594	Nothing's Moving - Major Problem
595	None Zip Zero
596	Is Your Ad Budget Going Up In Smoke
597	How To Choose The Best Affiliate Offer
598	The Licensing Loop
599	You Can Copy Me
600	We'll Test Your Ads
601	Make Funny Faces For 20 Minutes A Day
602	Road Mapping Your Business
603	Feats Of Productivity
604	Speak With Enthusiasm
605	The Missing Part Of The Equation
606	Don't Put It Off Any Longer
607	You Can Cancel At Any Time
608	Freebies Are A Hard Turn Down
609	Live That Role
610	Up A Creek Without A Paddle
611	More Information Smarter Decisions
612	Getting Started Is As Easy As 1-2-3
613	Save At Least 50-70% Today
614	This May Take Years To Play Out
615	Access Venture Capital Investors For Your Next Launch
616	Potential To Make Millions
617	The World's Biggest Bluff
618	Making Earned Money Online
619	Replace Bad Habits Fast
620	A Marketing Pecking Order
621	Kick Butt Business Ideas
622	That's What Makes Marketing So Great
623	The Fear Of Failure
624	What's In Store For You
625	Let Me Wet Your Whistle
626	Marketing Home Stretch
627	Living Below What You Can Bare

29

628	If Long Copy Stinks Think Soap
629	In The Ultimate Context This Has Huge Emotional Value
630	When The Options Are Endless
631	Help Me Take Control
632	Creating Camtasia Callouts
633	Try To Work In Isolation
634	Way To Go Broke Online Fast
635	Remember What Turns Prospects Off
636	Outside The Box Ideas
637	Change You Life This Weekend
638	Trace It To Fit Your Needs
639	Step Towards A Better Financial Future
640	Google Alerts
641	Does Your Site Need More Exposure
642	Tell Your Entire Story
643	Add Such A Sense Of Clarity
644	Spine Out Or Face Out
645	Did You Receive Your Share Yet
646	Quality Of Subscribers
647	Motivation Through Hardship
648	Maintain Eye Contact As Much As Possible
649	Inventive Empathy
650	Will You Be Naughty Or Nice
651	A Book Gives You Leverage That Encourages Change
652	Own Amazing Property
653	Popular Systems Integration
654	Get In Gear Explore New Roads To Wealth
655	Our Chosen Niche
656	Wrought By Technology
657	Punctuation Is Your Friend
658	Don't Quit - Get Started Right Now
659	Get Content Without Having To Write It Yourself
660	Great For All Parties Concerned
661	Guaranteed Lowest Prices
662	Toodles And Farewell
663	Money Is Like Water
664	Be Present And Vulnerable
665	Why Wealthier People Always Pay Themselves First

666	The Age Of Your Domain Matters
667	Keep A Straight Spine Position
668	We've Identified An Interesting Pattern
669	Say Yes To Every Opportunity
670	Life Isn't Always About Working For Other People
671	Make Your Kids Rich
672	Easily Manage And Update Your Army Of Affiliates
673	There's Limited Upside
674	Tips For An Irresistible Meeting
675	Nothing Will Be Untouched
676	I Had A Similar Experience
677	Looking For The Motherload
678	Free Enticing Offer Avoids Rookie Mistakes
679	Are Your Space Wasting Headlines Saying Nothing
680	Addicted To Shiny Objects
681	Monday Mayhem Mayday
682	What's The Fix
683	This Will Be Unlike Anything You've Ever Imagined
684	One Simple Change
685	This Is Your Homework For The Next 30-Days
686	More Money More Prosperity
687	Moments Of Glory
688	Monday Morning Marketing
689	Crank Out Winner After Winner
690	Getting The Nod From Sales And Marketing
691	This Is Nuts
692	Savvy Business Plan
693	How People Screw This Up All The Time
694	Hunt Down And Choose Just The "Right" Products
695	Remain Up To Date
696	Some See How The Big Boys Do It
697	Don't Mess With Another Man's Work
698	Forced Into Hiding
699	Simplicity Is The Key To Online Success
700	Why The Main Guys Won't Really Help
701	Avoid Resources That Drain Your Profits
702	Something Is Terribly Wrong
703	Hundreds Of Website Owners Are Signing Up

741	Ways To Sell Your Ad Space Like Crazy
742	Practice But Not Too Much
743	Eligible vs. Ineligible
744	People Will Follow You
745	Seeing Real Growth
746	Keep Changing
747	Largest List Of Big Profits Now Open
748	Push Your Conversions Sky High
749	We Compensate Innovation
750	Heard That A Gazillion Times Before
751	I Hate This Big Problem
752	I'll Show You Every Last Trick I Know
753	Allow For Transparency
754	Searching For Solutions
755	Are They Just Plain Idiots
756	Too Polished Can Be Too Cold
757	More Than Good Attentions
758	When They Find Value They Say YES
759	Everything Is On Sale
760	In An Age Of Materialistic Abundance
761	Point Your Domain Name To Your Page
762	Leverage Rising Internet Trends And Create New Streams Of Money
763	A Word From Our Network
764	The Four Step Approach To More Income
765	Inspire New Hires
766	What To Do When The Checks Aren't In The Mail
767	Just What We Expected
768	A Massive Difference
769	Coaching Is About Helping When Needed
770	Your Job May Be Next
771	I Know The Hot Spot
772	Bring It Anyway
773	Sitting On The Bench Isn't Taking A Very Big Risk
774	Unique Ways To Unlock Your Intuition
775	Changing A Reader's Opinion Requires Space
776	Using The Same Exact Method
777	Don't Go Broke

778	You Can Also Have Me On Your Team
779	Pop Out Headlines In Record Time
780	Just Got To Keep Going
781	Getting Hit With Reality
782	Be Praised And Admired
783	One Simple Mission
784	Serious Business Opportunity
785	Streaming Video Capture Ideas
786	Are You Willing To Multiple Your Business Every Year
787	Don't Get Lost In Details
788	Embracing A New Mindset
789	I've Always Had BIG Dreams
790	I'm Giving You Another Incredible Option
791	Here's The Short Version
792	Sell Premium Products & Services
793	Start By Scribbling Something
794	Don't Wait Too Long Because This Will Be CLOSING SOON
795	Once The Buzz Gets Going It's Doesn't Stop
796	Why They Will Never Beat This Price
797	Hire The Best For The Lowest Price
798	Spring Into Wisconsin
799	Perfect For Beginners
800	I Just Found These Amazing Training Tools
801	Transform Your Best Features
802	Invest In This Incredible Package
803	Look At All These Great Features
804	Take Everything You've Learned And Apply It To Their Needs
805	Bring Empathy And Caring
806	In Business And Lost It All
807	Light Your Marketing Fire
808	What An Eye Opener
809	Did He Just Go Overboard
810	No Frustrations
811	Sizzling Spring Sale
812	Don't Rationalize Make Excuses Or Point Fingers
813	There Really Is No Free Traffic
814	System Does All The Hard Work
815	Have A Website You Want To Accelerate

816	Video Setup Free Website
817	How Mid And Back List Authors Succeed
818	More Resources Than You'll Ever Need
819	Potential For Rebirth
820	This Is Better Than Posting A Job
821	The Internet Can Be A Scary Place Unless
822	Learn The Story At A Glance
823	Two Hours Of Marketing Is Nothing
824	Time To Start Cutting Costs
825	Money Pours Into Businesses Set On Autopilot
826	A Special Deal Just For You
827	Questions Are Our Pattern Of Language
828	Stand Out Better
829	Success In The Shortest Time Available
830	You Don't Need To Go Door To Door
831	Get Into Your Body
832	Hottest Topic For Discussion
833	Target The Right People
834	Make It Easier
835	Condition Yourself For Hope
836	Know The Secret
837	Add Some Value To Life
838	Generous Offer Won't Last Forever
839	Yours Totally Free
840	Most Basic Wealth Principle
841	Everyone With A Computer Is Trying
842	Boring But Useful Information
843	Come Across More Natural
844	How Serious Are You About Your Business
845	Destined To Change Our Industry
846	Entrepreneurs vs. Revolutionaries
847	Blotting Sheets And Face Powder
848	Sure You Can
849	This Is Where A Buyer Is
850	Lack Of Corporate Loyalty Requires A Backup Plan
851	Never Buy This
852	Whine Flu
853	Why 99.5% Of All Online Offers Aren't Being Honest

35

854	Making Marketing Information Easy To Digest
855	Pretty Toys At Any Price
856	Access Our Crystal Ball
857	Catching Up With An Old Friend
858	No Start Up Costs
859	The Secret Of Building A Great Team
860	Speak With Flowing Breath
861	Lift Your Finger Off The Order Button
862	Find Existing Continuity Offers
863	Learning The Hard Way
864	Place Your Free Ad On Our Ad Board
865	Niches Are Investments
866	It Must Require Less Than 1 Hour Of Your Time
867	Generating Bad Publicity
868	Not Too Big Or Too Small
869	The Main Cash Components Of Your Membership
870	Forget Waiting Months
871	Hope For Incredible Stupidity
872	Create Something Different
873	Health Wealth And Happiness Is Now Available
874	Finding Value To This Process
875	Everyone Is Ready To View Them
876	Congratulations You've Just Made Another Sale
877	Requires Little Editing
878	Grab Your Free Videos Now
879	Create A Happy Relationship With Your Money
880	RE: Account Closure
881	What's The Real Price You're Paying For Procrastination
882	Saving Time And Money
883	What Should I Wear
884	Remember When A Millionaire Use To Get Your Attention
885	It Shadowed My Every Waking Moment
886	Who Are You And Why Should I Listen
887	Nothing Like It Out There
888	Global Guidepost
889	Together We All Achieve More
890	Minimize Multitasking
891	Pouncing On Juicy Headlines

892	Maybe It's All The Craziness
893	Stop Paying Others To Install Your Scripts
894	Pick Up The Essentials
895	You Can See The Results Immediately
896	I've Got A Lot To Tell You About
897	A $100 Billion Dollar Industry And Growing In Any Economy
898	The Most Amazing Thing Of All
899	People Will Buy
900	Never Give Anything Away For Free
901	Never Be Disheartened
902	Generational Difference
903	This Is So Cool
904	Local Or Global Distribution
905	Bills Are Really Annoying Unless
906	I Report You Decide
907	What If The Lottery Came With A Guarantee
908	Start Writing Honest Reviews
909	Making Money Is Easy Keeping It Is Challenging
910	Intuition Says That There's Is Another Way
911	Avoid Hodgepodge Marketing
912	Opportunities Are In The Bag
913	Want To Change The World
914	Creating A New Reality
915	Simply Piece It Together Like A Puzzle
916	Getting A Bad Rap
917	The Most Advanced Technology On The Web
918	Recruit With Words
919	Can And Will Change Your Life
920	Bigger Than The Internet
921	Simple Changes That Make A Huge Difference
922	Here's A Plan For Success
923	Catching Errors
924	The Actual Performance
925	Increasing Everyday
926	Strategic Leverage Provides The Answers
927	What Happens When You Purposely Don't Mention Price
928	Not Just Instant Profit
929	Stable Income From Your Computer

38

967	The Perfect Exchange
968	Making The Most Of Your Insite
969	Find A High Search Keyword
970	Do People Trust Gurus
971	Rest Your Mind
972	Low Startup Cost
973	Give It A Read
974	Higher Quality Leads
975	The Answer Came To Me
976	Move Into The Happy Customer Arena
977	One Last Closing Thought
978	Appealing To The Millennial Generation
979	Why Am I Doing This
980	Not Naturally Gifted
981	Warm Up Your Voice And Body
982	Don't Be Burdened
983	Market Over A Period Of Time
984	Myth-Buster Tears You Apart
985	Everything You Need Is Set Up And Ready To Go
986	Everyone Will Be Rewarded
987	I'm Being Dead Serious
988	I Know Why You're Here
989	Won't Take Up Extra Time
990	Worried About Your Future
991	How To Handle Lost Sales
992	Six Pack vs. The Keg
993	My Business Made Me Rich
994	Silence The Naysayer Within
995	Dress In A Way That Is Authentic
996	Finding Something You Can Look Forward To
997	Never Cold Call Again
998	Kick Your Salesmanship
999	Don't Settle For Traffic Scraps
1000	Tracking Visitor Intelligence
1001	Know What You Really Want
1002	Work To Zero Work
1003	Making It Instantly Available
1004	This Site Could Be Banned At Any Moment

1005	Best File Compression Around
1006	Seeking More Exposure
1007	Building Schools In The Cloud
1008	Avoid Selling Passion
1009	Simple And Powerful
1010	I Know How
1011	Have All The Success You Could Ever Want
1012	Red Hot Tip
1013	Perfect Marketing Partners
1014	The Answer We've Been Looking For
1015	When To Feel Awesome
1016	Don't Kick Yourself In The Butt Over This Mistake
1017	Why Settle For Seconds
1018	Make Feeling A Broad Adventure
1019	Killer Marketer Stalks And Plots His Moves Effectively
1020	Take A Breath And Continue
1021	What's Your Innovation Capital Worth
1022	Amazing Sneaky Trick
1023	Redeem Your Coupon
1024	How To Create An Idea From Scratch
1025	Totally Tipsy Tuesday
1026	The Only Cost Is Storage Space
1027	Turn Your Computer Into An ATM
1028	We Look Forward To Helping You Master These Crucial Skills
1029	Sell Like You Mean It
1030	The Bombardment Will Continue
1031	Take Away The Risk
1032	All It Takes Is One Wrong Idea
1033	Create Your Own Income Generating Self-Perpetuating Techniques
1034	Compassionate Marketing Neighbors
1035	Shortest Email Ever
1036	Worried About The Economy - Start A Online Side Business
1037	The Simple Pleasures
1038	Don't Be A Business Wuzzbeen
1039	The Social Boom Has Been Lowered
1040	Double Your Profits
1041	Turnkey Marketing Systems That Fail Profitably
1042	It Happen At Starbucks

1043	Hear My Musical Collection
1044	Make A Lot More Money Than You're Making Now
1045	The Accidental Marketer
1046	Tour de Force Benefits Of Internet Marketing Unveiled
1047	EZ Money Makers Promote And Earn
1048	Critical Factors That Determine Your Success Online
1049	Marketing Brainstorms And Cash-Making Tactics
1050	Most Underrated Method Of Making Money
1051	Save Your Organization
1052	Virtual Doorway To Success
1053	Reading This Became A True Pleasure
1054	Nothing To Buy No Obligation
1055	How To Reap Huge Profits From Pre-Foreclosures
1056	Put A Heavy Book On Your Stomach
1057	Your Account Is Non-Active
1058	Article Marketing Makes Big Return
1059	Get Over There Now
1060	Get Paid
1061	Feeding The Need To Know
1062	Physical Emotional And Logical Conflicts
1063	Let's Get Into The Nitty Gritty
1064	Why I Saved My Head
1065	How Low Can You Go
1066	Limited Time Offer Don't Miss Out
1067	Will You Chop Your Video
1068	Unleash Your Inner Genie
1069	Double Your Enrollment
1070	For Those Who Can't Wait
1071	Bounce On Your Butt
1072	I Got Myself A Coach
1073	Twist Your Way To Trimmer Abs
1074	Be A Marketing Sampler
1075	How Many Of You Could Use This Now
1076	Not Just For Headlines
1077	Punch It Up Rather Than Punching Yourself
1078	This Fall's Hottest Offer
1079	Want To Advertise To Millions Legitimately
1080	Consumer Behaviors Are Changing

1081	Relax With Results
1082	Create Your Own Dream Life Style Here
1083	Facing A Long Hard Climb
1084	Most People Who See This Won't Even Try
1085	Let's Start Publishing Shift
1086	What Things Do You Power
1087	Enunciate Each Word
1088	Feast And Fun
1089	Has That Day Never Come
1090	Learn To Say It Differently
1091	Reassure Yourself You're Ready
1092	Ready For A Change
1093	Golden Goose Turns Customers Into Repeat Buyers
1094	Still Seeing Green
1095	There's Not A Lot Of Time Left
1096	Life Can Be Sweet
1097	How To Beat A Billion Dollar Company
1098	Having Inter-Operational Discord
1099	Sound's Pretty Amazing Doesn't It
1100	Godsent Miracles Happen When Least Expected
1101	The Personal Publishing Revolution
1102	Butterfly Ball
1103	Create A Robust Offer That Just Can't Be Refused
1104	Raise the Level of Competence
1105	I Love These Kinds Of Deals
1106	The Secret Will Shock You
1107	Kudos To All
1108	More Than One Way To Make Money
1109	Immune To Economic Downturns
1110	Let's Keep In Touch
1111	Boundless Ways To Anchor Down More Sales
1112	Let Me Introduce Myself
1113	Nice To Know - Looks Interesting But
1114	News vs. Announcing
1115	So There You Have It
1116	WAIT Why Am I Talking
1117	Why Am I Always Struggling To Make Money
1118	See How I Run My Multi-Million Dollar Business

1119	When Winning Becomes The Worst Thing That Happens In Vegas
1120	Secure From Hackers And Thieves
1121	Your Crystal Profit Ball
1122	Good Luck Relies Upon This Secret
1123	Redirect Boss
1124	Takes Next To No Work To Do
1125	Leading You In The Right Direction
1126	A Passionate Dream Is Much More Than A Possibility
1127	Look What I Just Bought
1128	Mini Site Profits
1129	Reach Your Goal Faster
1130	Start And Stop Your Sentence
1131	Look At It This Way
1132	Home Make Money Online
1133	Pre-Sell The Offer
1134	Most Important Step In Creating A Headline
1135	Priceless Road Map
1136	That's The Way It Was Designed
1137	Learn To Question Everything
1138	Justify Every Penny Spent
1139	Help Your Users Get Started Right Now
1140	How To Position Your Headlines
1141	Get Out There And Test It
1142	When Buy Is Bought
1143	Don't Let People Get To You
1144	Become Their Advocate
1145	Show Up Energized
1146	It's A Worthy Divergence
1147	Extremely Easy To Do
1148	Dominate Your Own Market Before It Disappears
1149	Richest Market On Earth
1150	You're Sure To Find What You Need Right Here
1151	Million Dollar Idea
1152	Give Me A List Of Your Favorite Movies
1153	My Secret Cash Strategies And Wealth Making Methods
1154	Offer Something Extremely Unique
1155	Even A Monkey Could Get Sign Ups Using This
1156	Sustainable Development

43

1157	Tweaked And Optimized To Perfection
1158	It's Just Because You Don't Know Where To Start
1159	Time Sensitive Opportunity
1160	Get The Full Story Here
1161	More Automation More Income
1162	Headlines Must Speak For Themselves
1163	My Affiliate Strategy
1164	Seven Figure Income
1165	30-Day Free Trial
1166	They'll Either Opt-In Or Die
1167	Men Respond To Money
1168	A Chance To Make Awesome Money On Autopilot
1169	You'll Be Thoroughly Blown Away
1170	They're Going To Give You Superficial Answers
1171	Stranded On Your Online Raft
1172	Quality Web Promotions
1173	Ensure A Seamless Blend
1174	Never Has Advertising Been So Profitable
1175	Why Editing Is An Investment
1176	Mark Your Calendars For May Madness
1177	Stop Hemorrhaging And Start Making Money
1178	1000's Of Clicks Per Hour
1179	Magic Money Multiplier
1180	My Special Discount Thank You Rate
1181	What's Your Angle
1182	You Don't Have To Fear Piracy
1183	Sources Of Profitable Niches
1184	Calibrating Your Money Tree
1185	The Power Of 25
1186	The Tipping Point
1187	How To Get "Future Money" Out Of Any Launch - Simple
1188	I Got Suckered In Big Time
1189	Geotargeting With Adwords
1190	They Will Listen To You When You Become The Expert
1191	Shocking New Strategy
1192	Are You One That Only Watches Things Happen
1193	Setup An Opt-In Email Capture Form
1194	Best Way To Offer Freebies

44

1195	The Key Is In How You Word It
1196	Being Lured Into Money Traps
1197	Organize Your Specific Tasks
1198	All About Just Making Money
1199	Even If You're Flat Broke
1200	Adrenalin Pumping
1201	When Dreams Are Dashed
1202	Freedom Of Information Is Changing
1203	I've Learned Many Ways To Fail
1204	Free Is Not Sustainable
1205	Magic Words Customers Love
1206	Define This Simple Term And Change Your Life
1207	Social Shenanigans At Work
1208	Maximize Your Opportunities Continuing The Journey While Other Stop
1209	I Want It Right Now
1210	3 Favorite Affiliate Programs To Share With Your Downline
1211	It All Depends On You
1212	The Average Stick Rate Is 9-14 Months
1213	This Winter's Hottest Offer
1214	Follow Your Dreams
1215	Created To Run Automatically
1216	This Is No Longer Just Theory
1217	Did Yesterday Really Happen
1218	Time To Start Building Your List
1219	Talking Head Videos
1220	Has Your ISP Website Been Shutdown
1221	The Only Person To Spend Your Time On
1222	How To Find A Market That's Perfect For You
1223	Listen To It Now
1224	You've Got To Know Your Stuff
1225	Finding Old Friends
1226	A Truly Unique Problem With A Quick Solution
1227	Who's Talking About You
1228	Why Lose When You Can Win
1229	How To Find A Money-Making Niche
1230	Most Problems Are Due To Miscommunication
1231	Compel And Seduce Your Decision Makers

1232	Here's All That Making Money Is
1233	Bamboo Glasses
1234	My Hobby Was Collecting Money
1235	Stay Within Your Gesture Frame
1236	Who Knew What This Little Button Could Do
1237	You MUST Act Now
1238	Zero Sum Game With Clear Winners
1239	Get Rid Of Those Constant Set Back Excuses
1240	People Hate To Be Sold
1241	Learn From The Best And Copy Them
1242	Make A Commitment To Act
1243	Will You Be Ready For This
1244	That's What I Want For You
1245	When The Answer Is YES
1246	It Set The Light Bulb Off
1247	Stunning Pay-Offs
1248	Speak For Your Stomach
1249	Super Affiliate Strategies
1250	Unlock The Secret To Accumulating Wealth
1251	Call Here And Receive A $10 Discount
1252	Dependable Monthly Income Generator
1253	Be Proud Of Your Product Or Service
1254	What's Your Social Media Edgerank
1255	Limping From One Crisis To Another
1256	It's Time To Make Your Choice
1257	Well Developed Goal
1258	Who Stole Your Bonus Check Today
1259	Show Me Your Skills
1260	Stimulate Your Thinking
1261	That's No Way To Make A Living
1262	Jaw Dropping Wonder
1263	Web Audio Waiting To Record Your Success Story
1264	K.I.S.S Need I Say More
1265	An Average Guy Who Knows What Works
1266	Why Are You Giving That Away For Free
1267	Results Other Got
1268	Why Customers Recommend Only Us
1269	Category Audios

1270	Unlock The Truth Behind More Traffic
1271	What Really Works Anymore
1272	From Puffery To Praise: How To Turn Hype Into Sales
1273	Opportunity Focus Time
1274	Effective Openings
1275	Deal Of The Week
1276	No Product Start With Bypass Surgery
1277	Talk Is Cheap
1278	Blistering Fast Delivery
1279	Don't Limit Your Life By Thinking What You Can Have
1280	You're Order Is On Its Way
1281	I'm Not Going To Place A Limit On Your Profits
1282	The School Of Getting It Done
1283	Just Like Telling A Story
1284	Fixing A Negative Image
1285	Category Scientific Advertising
1286	This Safelist Has Active Members Ready To See Your Ads
1287	Putting The Power Of Publishing In Your Hands
1288	The Question That Is Right In The Zone
1289	Subhead Your Links
1290	What If It's Not Engaging
1291	Unlock My Brain
1292	This Definitely Ranks Top Of The Marketing Charts
1293	Eliminate Stress And Anxiety From Your Life
1294	Stop Setting Goals To Achieve Success
1295	Marketing Landscape Changes
1296	Kickstart Your Greatest Dreams
1297	Reclaim Your Childhood
1298	Real Revenue Model
1299	Focus And Explain Your Business With Total Clarity
1300	Enjoy This In Your Car
1301	Pass The Vision
1302	Are We Really Alone Online
1303	Restore Your Focus
1304	Gravitate Toward Those Who Value Your Products
1305	Jumping From Program To Program
1306	Pay Per Action
1307	Are You Receiving Advanced Notification

1308	Take Your Game Online
1309	Don't Let Them Cut You Out Of Your Sale
1310	Online Money-Making Guide
1311	Beginner Or Veteran Who Haven't Figured It Out
1312	Why It Will Make You Wealthy
1313	Trying To Reclaim Your Image
1314	I Give Myself Goosebumps
1315	This Is Not A Get Rich Quick Scheme
1316	Are You Willing To Share Your Knowledge
1317	Let's Talk About The Marketing Of It
1318	Did You Receive My Email Or Should I Resend
1319	Define Success For Yourself
1320	Make Money Without Paypal
1321	Educated Out Of Creativity
1322	Learn From The Cloud
1323	Connecting With Real People
1324	Boost Your Energy
1325	Don't Miss This Again
1326	I Wanted To Send You This Sooner
1327	Bonus Baiting Affiliate Commissions On Steroids
1328	I'll Be Hooking You Up Today
1329	They're Even Giving Away Prizes
1330	How To Win The Battle
1331	One Begins Where One Is
1332	That Has To Be Sexier
1333	Awesome New Ad Site Plus Guaranteed Income
1334	You Can Never Have Too Much
1335	When Hard Work Pays Big Time
1336	Time And Resources
1337	Which Problem Do You Want To Beat
1338	Put Yourself In A Different Atmosphere
1339	The Biggest Bonus Of All
1340	Few Have A Clue
1341	Internet Marketers Hall Of Shame
1342	What Happens When You're Not Prepared
1343	Where To Do It Right
1344	Puppy Dog Licks
1345	Price Will Be Going Up

1346	Is Writing Too Tedious
1347	Milquetoast Marketing
1348	Three Tips For Finding Top Shelf Clients
1349	Website Feeling Embarrassed Lately
1350	Money Making Cravings
1351	Touching The Heart Of The Matter
1352	Different Marketing Techniques And Strategies
1353	Finding Bad Ass Products That Make Tons Of Money
1354	How Has Playing It Safe Made You Any Real Money
1355	How Do You Know When You Found The Right Solution
1356	Swipe File Examples
1357	We Want To Support Your Business
1358	Spare Time Money
1359	Looks Like You Ignored This Yesterday
1360	Don't Be Afraid To Blink
1361	We Have All You Need Here
1362	Why The Wizard Fried His Own Brain Waves Over This
1363	Who's Your Keyword Watchdog
1364	What Your Prospects Believe
1365	This Truly Made A Difference
1366	5 Steps To Come Up With 12 Product Ideas
1367	Reasons Why Successful Marketers Succeed
1368	Speak From Your Heart
1369	Multi Domain Usage
1370	Get Free Traffic Leads Through This Free System
1371	Stuck On What To Do Next
1372	Finally Something I Understand
1373	Make Sure Your Video Has Great Sound
1374	One Slice At A Time
1375	Have You Measured The Pulse Of Your Business Lately
1376	The Exact System Used To Earn Thousands
1377	Streamline The Workflow Of Your Email
1378	Build A Cash Spewing Empire
1379	Today You'll Cross A Threshold
1380	Definitely A Recipe For Bankruptcy
1381	Why Create Your Own Product
1382	Your Just Made The Cut
1383	Build Your List And Maximize Your Profits Using Traffic Exchanges

49

1421	Harpoon Their Eyeballs
1422	Great Content Great Price Great Bargain
1423	Getting One Action
1424	Serialize Many Pieces Of Your Content
1425	Generates A Lot Of Traffic
1426	$1 For Any Four Books
1427	Connect With The Floor To Your Feet
1428	The Plague Of Denial
1429	Simple Steps Anyone Can Follow
1430	Now To The Sales Page
1431	Take Your Step Forward
1432	Never Assume Anything
1433	Just Haven't Gotten Around To It Yet
1434	Sex Sells Or At Lease Allusions Does
1435	Use Them For Good And Not For Evil
1436	Score This Touchdown
1437	Exploiting Your Voice
1438	Prices Will Decline
1439	Time Tested Secrets
1440	Tangible And Emotional
1441	Do Your Keywords Matter Anymore
1442	What Customers Really Want From You
1443	Are You Sabotaging Your Own Website
1444	Sure Ain't Grandpa's Way Of Doing Things
1445	You Want To Talk Money
1446	Words Fly Fast Yet Images Linger In Your Mind
1447	Stimulate Their Sense Of Curiosity
1448	Handing Power Back To You
1449	This Could Be Our Little Secret
1450	The Ultimate Image
1451	Try Link Bait To Catch Customers
1452	Amazing Affiliate Reports
1453	Is This What You Asked For
1454	The Bonus Just Got Bigger
1455	Do Not Hesitate
1456	Selling To The Senses
1457	Tap Into The Story Well
1458	Never Make Another Cold Contact

51

1459	Innovate Your Business Model Now For Profitability
1460	The Leading Premise Of Wealth
1461	Speechless vs. Spellbound
1462	You're In For One Helluva Ride
1463	Think About What You Really Want
1464	Breaking Down Every Facet
1465	Creating A Road Map For Success
1466	Fast Action Bonuses
1467	Benefit From My Marketing Mistakes
1468	The Dirty Little Secret Worth Stealing
1469	Inside The Members Area
1470	The Real Shift In Marketing
1471	Outdrive Your Competitors
1472	Look Slim Trim And Fit
1473	Overly Shiny Lipstick Distracts
1474	Do A Price Check
1475	Being Over Promised
1476	Why Do We Need To Learn This
1477	You Can See The Whites Of Their Teeth
1478	Tired Of Being Bamboozled
1479	Short Sales Pages
1480	How To Profit From Seismic Changes
1481	A Vicious Circle Of Decline
1482	Good Stuff Is Becoming More Infrequent
1483	Reduce The Cost Of Marketing Experiments
1484	Do You Have Performance Chops
1485	The Best Kept Healing Secrets In The World
1486	Pro Active Phone Update Service
1487	Copy And Paste Then Money Flows
1488	Perfect For Sleeping
1489	Your Price For Getting Access To This Killer Program
1490	Sick Of Doing Everything Yourself
1491	No Fast Hand Movement
1492	Which Ones Would You Like Now
1493	Borrow Credibility
1494	Approved By Industry Leaders
1495	Need A Leash
1496	Outsourcing Can Be Tempting

1497	Alignment And Proximity
1498	Earn Big Bucks Online
1499	Verify Their Existence
1500	Puts You In Control
1501	Can't Can't Can't
1502	Are You Really Excited
1503	Why Reinvent - Just Improve
1504	Working At Home Without A Stubborn Boss
1505	Business As Usual Is Dead
1506	For People Who Never Start
1507	Optimize Your Efforts
1508	Classified Ad Sites That You Can Post Too
1509	No Standard Procedure
1510	The Real Big Secret
1511	Protect Your Software And eBooks
1512	Meet Your Match And Save
1513	People To Watch
1514	The Email That Changed My Life
1515	Exact Art Of Generating Unstoppable Income
1516	I Want You To Get Started Right Now
1517	Work Whenever You Want To
1518	Fulfill A Fantasy
1519	Getting Your Site Into The Hands Of Search Engines
1520	It's In Your Pocket
1521	Top 101 Tips Of The Day
1522	Remember Everything Is A Test
1523	Be Generous With Yourself
1524	Make A Case For The Product
1525	Identify Solutions To One Problem
1526	Stop Learning
1527	Consider This As A Blend
1528	All About My Early Failures
1529	Write Down The Daily Things You Want To Accomplish
1530	One Giant Event
1531	One Heck Of A Ride
1532	Hire A Robot To Make Your Sales
1533	I'm Back From Paradise
1534	Earn A Residual Profit For Life In Minutes

53

1535	Why Can't Everything Be So Easy
1536	Your New Career Is Calling
1537	Remarkable Point And Click
1538	Black and White Photos That Will Amaze Your Mind
1539	I Couldn't Wait To Get My Hands On These
1540	Contact Thousands Worldwide
1541	Honest Clear And Direct Marketing Techniques
1542	Scams Rip-Offs Hype And Half Truths
1543	Why You Need To Act Now
1544	Adapt It To Your Situation
1545	For Those Who Think You Can't
1546	Video Mobile
1547	Profit From Your Subscribers From The Moment They Sign Up
1548	The Real Value Of Money Time And Work
1549	How To Write So People Buy
1550	Unmatched In History
1551	Secrets Of Making Money
1552	One Thing At A Time
1553	Don't Over Complicate It
1554	Sell Only Things You Believe In That Work
1555	Get Into My Head And Under My Skin
1556	Letting Yourself Down
1557	New Way To Manage Your Game
1558	Only 10% Above Wholesale/Dealers Cost
1559	What Would You Like For Free
1560	This Is Too Important To Miss
1561	Stay The Course
1562	Is Competition Killing Your Affiliate Commissions
1563	Offers To Put On Your Buy Buttons
1564	No Connections No Skills
1565	Doesn't Require A Big Shift In Your Approach
1566	You Don't Have Space To Waste
1567	Start Talking With Your Prospective Customers
1568	How Much Money Can Be Made From This Activity
1569	Do Your Customers Know What They Want
1570	Your Newest Top Dollar Client
1571	Two Weeks To Success
1572	A No Nonsense No Obligation Approach

1573	No One What To Go Crazy
1574	The Niche Giveaway
1575	Deep Marketing Dive
1576	Leveraging Existing Stuff You Already Have
1577	Sure Fire Way To Get Ahead
1578	Did Their Headline Catch Your Eye
1579	Targeted So Well They Can't Help But Buy
1580	Still Pounding The Job Pavement
1581	Favors Have A Shelf Life
1582	But That Early Anticipation And Excitement Soon Dies Down
1583	Eliminating The Risk Of Loss
1584	Easy Payment Plan
1585	Supportive Social Networking
1586	Monetize Your Own Hot Content Ideas
1587	Looking For A Talented Team Working For You
1588	Huge Marketing Error
1589	Always Convey Your Principal Sales Point
1590	Experience Financial Freedom
1591	Grease The Pat To Excellence
1592	Explosive Revenue Campaigns
1593	Wholesale Video Game Sources
1594	Summer Into Wisconsin
1595	More Than Ever Thought Possible
1596	Gate Keepers Or Star Makers
1597	Three Word Style Statement
1598	Digital Bananas Forever Isn't A Slippery Adventure
1599	Reenter Your Request
1600	It's Bigger Than You
1601	My Top Plan Of Attack
1602	Here's Your Chance To Personally Meet Some Amazing Entrepreneurs
1603	Learn A Lot From This Approach
1604	Marketing Conversions Begin On Page One
1605	Answering Questions In A Timely Manner
1606	Anything You Want
1607	Taking Charge In A Struggling Economy
1608	Spring Marketing Catalog
1609	Quite Trying To Impress Your Audience

55

1610	Learning Stuff The Hard Way
1611	Make Money Tonight
1612	Don't Miss This Next Session
1613	Here Are The Important Questions To Always Ask
1614	Making Money The Easy Way
1615	Know The Business From Top To Bottom
1616	Place These Tasty Web Sites On Your Menu
1617	iAd Apple Mobile Ad Platform
1618	The Only Difference Between These Two Are Attitude
1619	Target All Your Niche Learners
1620	Mindsets Change Quickly With An Effective Coach
1621	It's Kind Of Just What We Do
1622	Information On Demand
1623	Start Unflattering Your Mind
1624	Bring On The Affiliates
1625	Fools Like To Complicate Simplicity
1626	Share Your Experiences To Draw People Closer Together
1627	Simplifying The Complex
1628	Watch The Magic Numbers Start Flying In
1629	Your Level Of Presence
1630	Pure Positive Energy
1631	Maybe You Won't Want To Go To Bed Just Yet
1632	Turnkey Domains For Sale Website
1633	More Likely To Happen Now
1634	True Or False - You Have Enough Money
1635	The Reason We Do This
1636	Create Killer Landing Pages
1637	Why 95% Go Bust
1638	Join The Team
1639	Want More Traffic
1640	The Problem They Are Trying To Solve
1641	Turning A Profit From Home 24/7
1642	Success Starts With Something Of Value
1643	Avoid Inner Conflict In Both
1644	Get A Freebie Just For You!
1645	Can You See Yourself Doing This
1646	It's Time To Make The Offer
1647	Elite Coaches And Mentors From Around The World

1648	Blow Conversion Rates Out Of The Water
1649	See Who Clicks
1650	Do The Math On The Results
1651	Avoiding High Risk Burn Out
1652	Category Selling
1653	Give Others A Chance To Deliver Ideas
1654	Why Do You Continue To Ignore Your Niche
1655	Love Your Body Language
1656	Focus Your Question On One Specific Subject
1657	Infamous Butterfly Ballot
1658	Ways To Propel Visitors To Your Order Page
1659	I Want To Make This As Simple As Possible
1660	Give Them Specific Directions
1661	Have An Instant Video Business
1662	Let's Seal The Deal
1663	Key Is How Serious Are You
1664	Get Something Extra
1665	No Story No Sale
1666	Engage Customer's Interest Longer
1667	Illusive Link
1668	Set Up Your Order Taking
1669	Category Copywriting
1670	Wealth Freedom And Success
1671	Do You Know What They Want
1672	Sold Out Within One Hour
1673	Looking For A Money Miracle
1674	Guarding Your Paycheck Keywords
1675	What's Your Million Dollar Plan
1676	Care To Join Us
1677	In Case It Wasn't Obvious
1678	What You'll Learn Once You Retire
1679	Make Money With Each Blink Of Your Eye
1680	Logic Is Only Based Upon Theoretical Prevention
1681	Stop Working So Hard Trying To Capture Traffic
1682	The Target Just Got Bigger
1683	Want A Free $500 Audit
1684	A Product that People Actually Need
1685	How Courage Gives You Power

57

1686	**4 Easy Steps**
1687	**Need A Photo Restored**
1688	**You Deserve To Know This As An Investment In Yourself**
1689	**Watch Your Earnings Skyrocket As You Learn**
1690	**You Know You Need Sub Headlines Tools**
1691	**Facebook Allows You To Build Lists**
1692	**Really Stupid Ideas**
1693	**Do You Clothes Date Your Video**
1694	**Seek Self-Promotion**
1695	**Making A Good Faith Effort**
1696	**Time To Tell The Truth**
1697	**Ask For Help**
1698	**The Age Of Pain Is Gone**
1699	**What's Your Unknown Story**
1700	**Become An Independent Advocate**
1701	**Sale Of The Millennium**
1702	**Five Easy Ways To Make Money From Your Blog**
1703	**FEAR Is A Dream Killer**
1704	**Google Translation; Translating Web Pages**
1705	**Makes My Job A Lot Of Fun**
1706	**Create A Position Hook**
1707	**Software Tells All**
1708	**Get Rich In Your Niche**
1709	**Predicting Search Volume**
1710	**I'm Not A Blind Beast**
1711	**Fast Action Rewards Bonuses For Decisive Members**
1712	**Let Me Put You At Ease**
1713	**Find The Time**
1714	**Active Imaginations Wanted**
1715	**They Will Buy Bundles**
1716	**Is Your Head Still Spinning**
1717	**All We Have Is Our Minds**
1718	**I Have A Direct Line To The Creator**
1719	**The I-tis Trap**
1720	**Working Without A Plan Is Doomed To Breed Failure**
1721	**Is Your Life Becoming A Soap Opera**
1722	**Quick Easy And Free To Use**
1723	**You Deserve A Real Opportunity To Enjoy Your New Profits**

1724	Build A Habit
1725	Love Your Offer
1726	The Key To Creating Headlines That Prospects Love
1727	Well Now You Can
1728	Distinct Immediate And On Going Solutions
1729	Come To The Garden With Your Shovel
1730	Giving To Those Who Need It The Most
1731	Sport Of The Ages
1732	Want To Push People's Buttons
1733	Simplicity Always Sells
1734	Change The Way You Think About Doing Business
1735	Get To Know And Love Characters
1736	You Want Them To Look At Your Face
1737	No Idea What To Do Next
1738	Maybe You're Not Tracking Well Enough
1739	Yes It's Here
1740	Wistful Tones
1741	Seriously Dude - It Just Doesn't Sleep
1742	I've Worked With Many Of Them
1743	The Advances Of Being Smaller
1744	Flashbacks On Success
1745	Use This Secret Responsibly
1746	Lead With One Close With One
1747	Digital Heaven On Earth Is Yours For The Taking
1748	Tie It Into Urgency And Scarcity
1749	Making The Right Move
1750	Create Unlimited Categories And Subcategories
1751	Make Windows XP Shut Down Faster
1752	What Everybody Ought To Know About This Business
1753	Think About It
1754	Automatically Incorporated Into This System
1755	Free To Find Out
1756	These Will Not Make You Rich
1757	Support Vendors Waiting To Become Affiliates
1758	How About A 5 Day Trial On Us
1759	Get It Listed For Free
1760	Don't You Deserve To Be Next
1761	Comes With A Full 100% Guarantee

1762	Website Design Keys That Help You Sell
1763	The End Result Is Worth It
1764	The Impact It Deserves
1765	Why Quibble
1766	This Is Not A JOB
1767	Not Bad At All
1768	Concepts Tested And Proven
1769	How Much More Productive Are You
1770	Do You Know What Really Excites Me About This
1771	Will They Stop And Read
1772	A Handful Of Trusted Friends
1773	There's No Reason Why It Shouldn't Be You
1774	What We Do Is Sell Them What They Want
1775	Your Marketing Solution
1776	Survey Their Wants And Needs
1777	Here's Your Assignment For The Week
1778	Trying And Still Failing
1779	Is Your Work Very Intense
1780	29 Easy Web Design Tricks
1781	A Direct Challenge
1782	How About Brainstorming This One
1783	Use Red Paint In Section 17
1784	If You Order Now You'll Receive Everything Listed Below
1785	Becoming A Great Manager
1786	What Highly Innovative People Seek
1787	Make Your Spouse And Your Kids Happy
1788	Failure To Probe
1789	Profitable Shortcuts To Sustainable Online Business
1790	Are You Working Yourself To Death
1791	Unconditional Traffic
1792	Want More Time For Enormous Wealth Fun And Excitement
1793	Build Your Own Information System
1794	Free Shopping Genie
1795	Requires One Simple Thing called ACTION
1796	New Travel Benefits Included
1797	You're Now The Bank
1798	You've Got Me Live One On One
1799	Encourage Others To Innovate For You

60

1800	Dress Your Website For Success
1801	Test Your Website Now
1802	More Buy Buttons More Profit
1803	Years Ahead Of The Competition
1804	Create Your Own High Ticket eClass
1805	Just Announced For The Very First Time
1806	Analyzing Customer Data For Clues
1807	Did You Forget Your Own List
1808	Building Better Brains
1809	Now Reason To Be Anxious
1810	Charge 1/10 Of Your Price
1811	Internet Marketing Integration
1812	Providing Simplicity And Precision
1813	100 Percent Financing
1814	How Much Rejection Can You Take
1815	Offer Them A Decision
1816	Isn't It Time You Turned Things Around
1817	Real Truth About Multiple Income Streams
1818	Create Lasting Evergreen Income
1819	The Fastest Way To Making Millions
1820	Work For Yourself
1821	Without A Huge Payoff Why Bother
1822	There's Got To Be A Better Way
1823	Top Minds Think Alike
1824	Give Value Before You Sell
1825	Front Row Seat To Your Own Success
1826	Implement My System
1827	Speak With Empathy
1828	Wage Your War Against Fear
1829	I Couldn't Take It Anymore
1830	May I Send You A Free Gift
1831	Begging For A Solution To What You Really Want
1832	Make The Cash You Deserve
1833	Going Broke Was The Greatest Day Of My Life
1834	Stop And Do It Now
1835	Good That We Found You At Last
1836	Never Forget About Your Customers
1837	Seal Of Approval

1838	A Simple But Powerful Web Site
1839	Headlines Are Scary If Not Memorable
1840	Why Minds Attempt Deception
1841	Ad Campaign That Makes Huge Money
1842	Score Real Savings
1843	Pass The Look Test
1844	Drink Lots Of Water
1845	Increases Innovation And Production Methods
1846	I Had No Idea Of What I Was Doing
1847	Laying The Groundwork
1848	But That's Not You, Right
1849	This Market Is Truly Massive
1850	Online Marketing Screener
1851	100% Of Our Members Make Money
1852	Wise Choice Wise Decision
1853	Who Said Size Doesn't Matter
1854	Make Them Feel Great
1855	Do The Walk Around
1856	Give Your Joint Venture Offer An Extra Punch
1857	I've Really Got Your Number
1858	Jealousy Envy And Pain
1859	Products Which Produce The Most Money
1860	What's The Cycle Of Your Website Visitors
1861	Selected And Complied Just For You
1862	Why Does This Make Me Money
1863	Grab Their Subconscious Mind First
1864	Boldly Coming To Your Aid
1865	When You Focus On A Goal Measurement Will Be Powerful
1866	Zombie-Killing Tactic
1867	Lost Key Retrieval
1868	Internet Marketer Hit By Headline
1869	Trying To Figure It All Out Sucks
1870	Investing In Niches
1871	When A No Becomes Yes
1872	Are Zombies Killing Your Profits
1873	Help Us Build A Virtual Village
1874	You Can Just Copy What They Did
1875	Clean Freak

1876	A Successful Turnaround Depends On You
1877	A Fairytale Business
1878	It's Time To Get The Whole Story
1879	Master The Millionaire Language
1880	I Have This Spreadsheet
1881	Specific Patterns That Create Success
1882	Let Me Show You How For Free
1883	Stimulate Your Brain With Fun Time
1884	Instantly Create Massive Waves Of Free Traffic
1885	Take Advantage Regardless Of Your Circumstances
1886	You And I Have A Lot In Common
1887	You Have A Right To Be Heard
1888	Marketing Deliverables
1889	Some Secret Success Sauce
1890	When Two Souls Unite It's Magical
1891	Praised For Our Marketing Innovations
1892	Santa Wanted Christmas To Coming Early
1893	Mesmerizing Sales Presentations
1894	Sorry Boss But You're Fired
1895	Please Note - The Master Is In
1896	When Did Your World Begin
1897	Why Didn't You Market Today
1898	Take Your Time
1899	Free Trial
1900	Hot Products
1901	Experience The Power Of Marketing
1902	Stories Sell Stuff
1903	You Get Over $1200 In Bonuses
1904	My Step-By-Step Screen Shots
1905	Take Fear Out Of Buying
1906	Bite The Silver Bullet
1907	Are You A Big Believer
1908	Building Influence With Free Membership Sites
1909	Google Chrome Installation
1910	Make A Realistic Plan Of Action To Follow
1911	Winter Sale Now Heating Up
1912	Ultimate Source Of BUZZ Leverage
1913	No Cost Resource

1914	Your Current Predicament
1915	Setup A Squidoo Lens That Helps Bring In Money
1916	So Powerful You Think You're Cheating
1917	What If You Could Find The Perfect Prospects
1918	Members Pay You Money Just To Join For Free Today
1919	Find Locate And Acquire
1920	Time To Make It Rain
1921	Always Pay Yourself First The Bills Will Still Be There
1922	Hold Your Breath For A Moment
1923	Networking Like The Pros
1924	Why There's Scarcity Of Profits
1925	Don't Cheat Yourself Treat Yourself Instead
1926	Here's The System In A Nutshell
1927	Use This And You'll Be Unbeatable
1928	Draw People In With
1929	I Teach By Doing
1930	Aren't You Glad You Asked
1931	Thoughts That Destruct
1932	Make Sure You Open This Web Page
1933	Marketing Co-Worker Needed
1934	No Hassles Refund
1935	Young Ones Like New Ideas
1936	Forget Stuffy DVDs And Home-Made Videos
1937	Sometimes The Lead Story Doesn't Make The Headlines
1938	Delivered Directly To Your Desktop
1939	Higher Archive Of Needs
1940	Don't Stand On The Sidelines
1941	One Of A Kind Program
1942	Are You Really Prepared To Handle A Flood Of Orders
1943	See A Whole New Perspective On Effective Marketing
1944	It Really Simplified Success
1945	Don't Forget One Time Money Offers
1946	Get Your Hit Counter Spinning
1947	IMPORTANT: READ THIS NOW
1948	Most People Fail To Grab The Opportunity
1949	Survey vs. Focus Group
1950	Don't Go Into Business Until You Memorize Them
1951	Hit Them At The Hot Point

1952	Here's The Scoop
1953	But Wait Till You Hear This
1954	Make Money Today - Get Started Now
1955	Know What You're Getting Into
1956	In Fact It's Downright Simple
1957	Take The First Step Toward Your Dream
1958	Ways To Earn Extra Money
1959	Piracy Is Free Advertising
1960	If There's A Money Back Guarantee More Sales Occur
1961	Transmit That Recognition
1962	Classic Polished Edge
1963	Meet The New Boy In Town
1964	I've Just Sweetened This Deal Big Time
1965	Internet Explorer Market Share
1966	This Ain't Chump Change
1967	Putting In The Time And Effort
1968	I Have A Marketing Riddle For You
1969	You Ever Felt CONFUSED
1970	You Really Don't Want To Get This Wrong
1971	Hating To Lose
1972	Much More Than Meets The Eye
1973	Making Stuff Faster
1974	Uncover Profitable Markets Not Yet Recognized
1975	Offer Ends Soon
1976	Certainly Gets People's Interest
1977	Never Be Afraid Of Failure
1978	We Hate Negative Thinking
1979	No More Worries
1980	Products You Want With Links
1981	As We Speak Email Is Dying
1982	Not So Flattering Nickname
1983	Powerful Component #3
1984	The Internet Is All About Advertising
1985	These Psychological Triggers Make People Buy
1986	Want To Expose Your Website
1987	Want To Be A Money Guide
1988	Avoid Loud Patterns
1989	So Why Do I Go Deep Like This

1990	Your Message Arrives In Only Seconds
1991	Learn To Fight Back
1992	Can't Sit And Watch Anymore
1993	Yours For Free Right Now
1994	Wouldn't You Like It Now
1995	Huge Well Defined Dreams
1996	Get Started On The New Path To Life
1997	Not Many Know About This
1998	I Want To Spoil You
1999	Testing An Idea Is Crucial To Fine Tuning Results
2000	Are You Insane A Lifetime Money Back Guarantee
2001	When Silence Is Golden
2002	$1000 In Coupon Savings
2003	No Techno Babble Here
2004	Refocus Setbacks
2005	Watch Your Lame Competition Become Envious
2006	Playing With Your Joy Stick Just Got Better
2007	Launch Your Own Grass Roots Campaign
2008	We Can Help Who You Are
2009	It Will Disappear Soon
2010	How Are These Problems Secretly Driving Your Life
2011	CAVEAT What Works And What To Avoid
2012	The Best Of The Best
2013	Essential Sparkplug For Marketing Ignition
2014	A Startling Epiphany
2015	Why People Have Problems With This Step
2016	Writing An Effective Press Release
2017	Asset Deficient Website Draining Your Future
2018	Know Where You're Going
2019	Lying On The Beach Soaking Up The Rays
2020	Simply Saying WOW Is The New Normal
2021	The Single Piece That Made The Entire Puzzle Make Sense
2022	Furious Price Hikes
2023	The Big Dream Killer - EXCUSES
2024	Make Your Point Bold And Clear
2025	Don't Let People Guess What To Do
2026	If You Can Do This Process
2027	The Exact Blueprint To Follow

2028	Pierced By 301 Nails And Retains Full Air Pressure
2029	Bring On Your Biggest Result
2030	Turn To The Future Now
2031	This Is All Part Of The Journey
2032	Pass This On
2033	I Just Found This Niche
2034	Social Networking Expands Your Empire
2035	What Works The Best
2036	How To Win With A Strategy
2037	What - No Agenda
2038	Would You Rather Be Rich Or Wealthy
2039	Be Your Own Niche King Of The Hill
2040	Always Provide Real Time Stats
2041	If You Do Kindle Consider This
2042	Earn Online Income
2043	A Glimpse Into Tomorrow
2044	When Length Of Domain Registration Matters
2045	Your Ads Are Your Lifeline To True Success Online
2046	The Value Chain Is Broken
2047	Stretch Your Lists Beyond Limitation
2048	Unlimited Source Energy
2049	No Over Scripted Here
2050	Earn A Track Record
2051	Squashing Sunday Sadness
2052	I Wish I Could Give You A Hug
2053	No Sponsoring Needed
2054	What Pay Per Click Advertising Is And How It Works
2055	Delivery Failure Notifications Limiting Your Profits
2056	A Lead Generating System Focused On Converting Sales
2057	It's All About Possibilities
2058	Fall In Love All Over Again
2059	Give People A Reason
2060	With The Right System It's Very Easy
2061	Click For Credits
2062	Lost Money I Didn't Even Know About
2063	Jump Start Your Creativity
2064	What Happened Immediately
2065	We Warned You To Join Us

67

2066	My Hand In Friendship
2067	Service And Patriotism
2068	Nothing To Lose
2069	It's Like A Personal Assistant
2070	This Is A Must-Watch
2071	Grow It Into An Empire
2072	This Expense Is No Longer Required
2073	The Niche Always Starts With A Need
2074	Prominent Bullets
2075	Organic Search Results
2076	First In And Last To Leave
2077	Logic Justifies Emotion Emotion Drives Sales
2078	Jumping Dangerous Hoops
2079	All Of Us Have These Common Problems
2080	Reset Your Industry
2081	Would A Conversion Rate Of 70% Be Of Interest
2082	What's Inside Your Business
2083	Build A Sticky Blog
2084	What's Your Digital Weakness
2085	Brimming With Incredible Information
2086	Cut Your Risks To Zero
2087	On Time And Below Budget
2088	More Than Casual Contemplation
2089	It's A Good Idea To Register
2090	Work That Is More Fulfilling
2091	Next Stop Nowhere
2092	Think Less Accomplish More
2093	Learning To Walk Before You Run
2094	These People Know The Truth
2095	Reap The Rewards From My Efforts
2096	Learn How To Sell Your Product
2097	Watch Your Niche
2098	Time Management Tips
2099	Now That's What We Call Turnkey
2100	Promoting Growth And Expansion
2101	Make A Fortune With Cutting Edge Technology
2102	My Girl Friend Hates This
2103	Add This Site To Your Favorites

68

2104	Doing All The Right Things
2105	We Just Can't Help It
2106	Are They Shutting Down Your IPO Again
2107	Read What Real People Think
2108	Consumers Will Beg You To Take Their Money
2109	It's A Crime
2110	Call Me Crazy But This Insane Offer Is Absolutely Free
2111	Maybe You're Worrying Too Much
2112	Jobless And Directionless
2113	Make Eye Contact
2114	I'm Ready To Give You The Push You Need
2115	One Simple Strategy
2116	Claim Hidden Keys That Open Doors
2117	The Ease Factor
2118	The Freedom To Work In Your PJs
2119	Ramp Up Your Online Business
2120	Your VIP Application Form
2121	Surprise And Engage Your Audience
2122	Two Versions Of The Truth
2123	For Your Self Esteem
2124	The Big Question Still Left Unanswered
2125	Instant Buzz For Your Site
2126	Test Website Colors
2127	Fighting So Hard To Sell
2128	How To Start Success
2129	Thanks For Sharing This With Your List
2130	Get The Deal In Writing
2131	Dramatically Accelerate Hot Product Sales
2132	Attract Exact Targeted Audiences
2133	Most Brilliant Group Of Minds Ever Imagined
2134	Create Your Mission Statement
2135	You've Just Finished Saving For Your Kids' College Fund
2136	Is Your Site A Serious Contender
2137	The Key To Separating Yourself From The Crowd
2138	Suck vs. Awesome
2139	Free Social Media Marketing
2140	Get Your Special Discount Now
2141	Efficient Disciplined And Systemized

2180	Creating A Larger Purpose
2181	All Season Long
2182	Faith Family Friends Fun And Financial Freedom
2183	Principles Of Change
2184	Is The Corruption Over
2185	As Long As It Needs To Be
2186	I Want To Show You The Real Process
2187	Being Bold Increases Response
2188	Tell Us What You're Thinking
2189	Baring All Doesn't Mean Getting Naked
2190	Baby Boomers On Fire
2191	There's No Way The Reader Can Lose Focus
2192	What Are You Looking To Leave Behind
2193	Inefficiently Priced Market
2194	Vital-Profits For Free Ads
2195	Why People Want To Be Sold
2196	Seven Dollar Solution
2197	What's The Ideal Goal That You Would Like To Achieve
2198	A Round Of Applause
2199	Making Money Blogging For Dollars
2200	Even Distributors Are Feeling The Pinch
2201	Choose The Approach Best For You
2202	Systems Have More Perceived Value
2203	The Art Of Solving Problems
2204	Purging My Way To Freedom From Email Clutter
2205	From A Successful Vantage Point
2206	Healthy Niches That Make Money
2207	The Best vs. The Rest
2208	Being Here Today Is Perfect Timing
2209	On Top Of Everything
2210	Lead The Way
2211	Showing A Softer Side
2212	Special Introductory Trial
2213	Make Decisions On How To Live Your Life
2214	Is Pinnacle Leadership Dying
2215	SEO Ranking Recipes
2216	What Comes To Mind
2217	Won't Nearly Cost You As Much

71

2218	It's No Longer Enough
2219	A Little-Known Tactic
2220	Join This New Gold Rush Opportunity Today
2221	Uploading Files To Your Server
2222	Plan For Growth
2223	How To Use Twitter To Crank Up Your Promo Power
2224	Free This Weekend
2225	Breathe Sleep And Dream Of Marketing
2226	You Can Stop Typing
2227	Large Scale Mastermining
2228	Easy Uploads To Your PC
2229	Guaranteed To Work
2230	The Best Kept Secret In
2231	How Many Times Have You Asked Yourself
2232	Upgrade Your Necktop Computer
2233	Everything Is Just Fine
2234	Testing Your Secret Cross Sells
2235	Any Affiliate Programs You Want
2236	Instant Opt-in Profits
2237	These Strategies Are Different
2238	Time To Turn People On
2239	Everyone Has A Unique Story To Tell
2240	Your Website Has Been Suspended
2241	I Expect This Offer To Go Very Quickly
2242	Wandering Aimlessly
2243	Value Added Service
2244	Marketing Face Value
2245	How Most People Screw Up Their Headlines
2246	Bridge The Gap To Wealth
2247	It Just Can't Get Any Easier
2248	We've Hired The Best Developers
2249	Friday Fortune Frontiers
2250	Send $.75 To Help Cover Postage And Handling
2251	Easiest Way To Get Your Products Online
2252	Want To Create A Software Empire
2253	When Can You Start
2254	Are They Saying No Deal To Your Ads
2255	What Happens When You Focus On Just Bad Stuff

72

2256	Don't Miss Monday
2257	Attacking The Marketing Day
2258	So Let's Get Started
2259	Why Develop A Friendly Long Term Relationship
2260	Time's Running Out
2261	Your Choice Continue To Struggle Or Shine
2262	Taste Your New Business
2263	Open Your Ears And Fill In The Blanks
2264	Don't Be Seduced By Distractions
2265	I've Personally Tested It
2266	Don't Outsource Your Marketing And Sales
2267	Click Here To Get My List
2268	Simply Learn More Here
2269	Hit Every 3-Point Shot
2270	You Can Use My Entire Staff
2271	Knowing How To Help Them Get Through Their Own Fears
2272	A Very Special Holiday Gift
2273	Motivated To Take Action
2274	Those Guys Suck
2275	Want To Get In Your Own Business
2276	Modular Concepts Called Knowledge
2277	Be More Beautiful
2278	This Is One Of The Few
2279	Funny Freakday Friday
2280	Does This Make You Look Strange
2281	Over The Next Few Days You'll Receive
2282	Lacking A Solid Commitment
2283	Powerfully Renewing
2284	Guaranteed For 100 Years
2285	A Decade Of Growth
2286	It's A Great eBook
2287	Loopholes That End Up Ripping You Off
2288	Bombed And Down
2289	Technical Developments That Can Hinder Success
2290	Transferable Private Label Rights
2291	This Is How It All Weaves Together
2292	Sorry It Just Sold Out
2293	Give Each Section Their Own Headline

73

2294	Sling This Into Your Wallet
2295	Completely Sold Out In Minutes
2296	Today's Dream - Tomorrow's Reality
2297	Find Yourself First
2298	So What's The Real Secret
2299	Pecking Order Superstitions
2300	A Full Expression Of Who You Are
2301	Eliminate Hassles And Tribulations
2302	Let Machines Sell Your Products
2303	May Commission Payment
2304	Thinking Of You
2305	Why Watch Streaming Video Free
2306	Rethink Your Current Situation
2307	I Find Myself Reviewing The Material Over And Over
2308	Fine Tune Your Elevator Pitch
2309	We've Perfected A System
2310	Is This A Myth Or Secret
2311	Why Employment Sucks
2312	Let's Take A Quick Break
2313	Hardcore Copywriter
2314	What's Relevant To Your Business
2315	Earn Income 24 Hours A Day 7 Days A Week
2316	Someone Is Fibbing
2317	10 Boundless Ways To Anchor Down More Sales
2318	Optimized For Color
2319	This Is Very Different
2320	Lead The Best Team
2321	Talk To 10 People In Your Related Niche
2322	Building A Test Bed Tool
2323	Are You The Cultural Warrior
2324	Everything Matters
2325	How To Put Up A Website
2326	Is Your Opt-In List A Joke
2327	Achieve An Appropriate Boost
2328	It's Bonus Time
2329	The Unrefined Multi-Tasking Wasteland
2330	Non-Functional Decoration
2331	When You Can't Find A Cure

2332	Get A Fresh Idea Every Day
2333	Tip The Scale For Your Prospects
2334	Change In Perception
2335	This Will Start To Change Things
2336	There Are Only 24 Hours In Today
2337	Making Money On Internet
2338	Make It Jump Off The Page
2339	Huge Discount For The First 100 Buyers
2340	This Is A Pack Of My Best
2341	Is Your Pot Of Gold Empty
2342	Tasks Well Suited
2343	A Real Business Guide For Entrepreneurs
2344	Don't Summarize What You Just Said
2345	More Bills Because You're Earning More Money
2346	Start Small
2347	I've Been Where You've Been
2348	People You Sponsor
2349	No Longer Tethered
2350	How To Dig Your Way Out
2351	By The Bucket Full
2352	Why They Stopped Justifying Mistakes
2353	Why Just Pick The Low Hanging Fruit
2354	Listen To The Video Script
2355	Show They You've Been There
2356	Being On Camera Is A Skill
2357	Before The Internet Existed
2358	Enjoy The Satisfaction It Produces
2359	I'm Not Talking About That
2360	Dramatically Boost Your Sales
2361	Don't Put This Off Till Tomorrow
2362	Triumph Over Adversity
2363	Traffic Is The Marketing Lifeblood
2364	An Irresistible Idea You Can't Ignore
2365	Begin Ruling Your Mind
2366	Web Army Knife
2367	I Really Hope This Helps
2368	Just Coasting To Retirement
2369	This Can Easily Blow Up In Your Face

2370	Consider Your Reaction When You Land On A Squeeze Page
2371	Fast Fantastic And Free
2372	Can You Spell N-O B-R-A-I-N-E-R
2373	How To Set Up Your Own Membership Site
2374	Say No If You Must But You'll Regret It
2375	Truly Simple Solutions For Complex Problems
2376	Design It Yourself
2377	Some Call This The Google Bounce
2378	New Search Navigation
2379	Timing Is Everything Act Now And Grab Your Free Bonus
2380	Creating Your Own Reality
2381	Imagine There's No Food In Your Marketing House
2382	Busy Days Are Here Again
2383	These Results Were Astounding
2384	Steal This Ebook
2385	Super Design Tricks
2386	A Day That Can Really Change Your Life
2387	Why Isn't This Taught In Kindergarten
2388	Your Only Goal Is Creating Useful Valuable Information
2389	Want To Strike It Rich In The Internet Gold Rush
2390	Free $500 Victoria Secret CPA Offer
2391	Failure By Trial And Error
2392	Idea Solution For People Out Of Work
2393	Thanks Guys And We'll See You Soon
2394	Maximize Your Income
2395	Your Affiliate Tool Box
2396	I Finally Found A Real Advertising Offer That Works
2397	Training On How To Succeed Online
2398	We Have Great Deals On Most Everything
2399	Hidden Legacy
2400	Does Product Creation Scare You To Death
2401	Are Your Secondary Headlines Equally Powerful
2402	Creativity Ingenuity And Entrepreneurship Will Fail Without This
2403	Instantly Become More Productive
2404	Ready To Finally Take Action
2405	The Force Behind The Headlines
2406	What Doesn't Get Done
2407	What Is Its Motivation

2408	Let's Tackle The Issue Of Time
2409	SEO Collateral Damage
2410	Fun Ideas Flooding The Mind
2411	Consumption Matters
2412	This Pet Needs A Second Chance
2413	Huge Research Surprise
2414	Tactics For Niche Broadcasting
2415	Your Patience Is About To Be Massively Rewarded
2416	Scarcity Drives Customers
2417	A Whole Lot Of Fun In The Machine
2418	Walk On Water For Your Prospects
2419	Products You Want
2420	Cheat Sheet For Generating Leads
2421	What Is That Thing You've Learned To Solve Their Need
2422	Turning Profits Into Real Money
2423	No Fluff No Filler No Fine Print No BS
2424	Say Your Name
2425	The Early Click Gets The Order
2426	Free Line Content
2427	What Were You Expecting - Fluff
2428	Earn More Tomorrow
2429	A Word Of Warning
2430	In A Nutshell
2431	Turns Clicks Into Commitment
2432	Here's An Idea
2433	Copywriting And Editing
2434	Programs Products And Services Started By Listening To Needs
2435	Focus On The Most Powerful 20%
2436	Tend To Lose Track Of Time
2437	I Don't Want To Work Like A Dog - Do You
2438	100% Profit Margin
2439	That Would Be Really Great
2440	Like Some Tools To Help
2441	Take Responsibility For Mistakes And Move Forward
2442	We're Even Going To Sweeten The Deal
2443	Avoid Bait And Switch Methods
2444	Turn Your Marketing Frown Upside Down
2445	Know Who The Enemy Is

2446	Customized To Meet Your Needs
2447	What's Your Reality Habit
2448	Don't Give Away Future Royalties
2449	Add More Personality And Resonance
2450	It's Not In The History Books Yet
2451	You've Asked For It
2452	Mind Map Mining
2453	I Cannot Say Enough
2454	It's About Time
2455	Is It Bonus Time Already
2456	It's Something We Have To Practice And Do Ourselves
2457	Extra Income Online
2458	There's Nothing Wrong With Money
2459	Brilliant Simplicity At Work
2460	You Won't Let This Slip Away
2461	Unedited Testimonials
2462	Barely Inhabit Your Body
2463	Send Your Words Upwards And Outwards
2464	When You Demand Extraordinary Service
2465	How They Earned Cash Without Technical Skills
2466	Deadly Infiltration Tears Down Conversion Resistance
2467	Fuel Your Passion
2468	People Spend More On Their Car Than Their Brain
2469	How Do You Find Lasting Happiness
2470	Show Me The Features
2471	F. Y. E. O.
2472	A Very Active Safelist - Join Now
2473	WOW Guess What Happened
2474	Would You Know If You Saw It
2475	Avoid Fashion Fad Clothing
2476	This Can All Be Yours
2477	Stunning Success Without Frustration
2478	Still Working For Peanuts
2479	They Order More Than They Can Sell
2480	Reveal Details About Yourself
2481	Miss It Or Miss Out
2482	Open Our Marketing And PR Folders
2483	Statute Of Limitation

2484	Let Me Squeeze Your Page
2485	Count Your Umm And Aaahs
2486	How To Get Floods Of Free Traffic
2487	Jump Start Ideas
2488	This Is Where Everything Is Heading
2489	3 Myths Of Successful Marketing Online
2490	Exclusive Never-Before-Released Set Of Videos
2491	Compensated Only On Results
2492	More Than Just A Slight Edge
2493	Get Better To Grow Larger
2494	Achieved Millionaire Status
2495	Ever Tried Singing For Your Supper
2496	Moving A Blog To Your Own URL
2497	You Gotta See This
2498	This Is A Massive Market
2499	Guru Doubler
2500	How To Survive Any Storm In The Economy
2501	Earn Money With Your Computer
2502	The Compelling Essence Of Making Money
2503	Is Success About Manipulating People
2504	Casual Smart And Modern
2505	Shock Till They Drop
2506	Everybody Sings The Blues Sometime
2507	Essential To Human Reasoning
2508	Ugly Ad Will Out Pull A Pretty Ad
2509	The Shock Doctrine
2510	Finding Lost Customers
2511	Peripheral Players In Marketing
2512	Grateful You Bought My Book And Actually Read It
2513	These Are All High Quality Downloads
2514	Benefit From A Robust Online Economy
2515	Rewriting History
2516	Keep Your Brand Natural
2517	The Important Keys To Success
2518	Find Great Deals Everyday
2519	Article Directory
2520	Less Than Half Price
2521	Who's Buying This

2522	Old Digital Trash
2523	We See I To Eye
2524	The Digital Revolution Is Already Here
2525	Benefit Layden Bullets Are What Sell The Product
2526	A New Millionaire Is Created Every Hour Are You Next
2527	Quickest Way To Achieved
2528	Create A Powerful Free Gift
2529	How To Stop Your Divorce
2530	Here's A Run Down Of What's Included
2531	The Size Of Audience Doesn't Matter
2532	Are You Really Ready To Become An Entrepreneur
2533	Here's My Objective
2534	Eliminate Fears Holding You Back
2535	The True Role Of Entrepreneurs
2536	Features Tell But Benefits Sell
2537	Make Sure Customers Have A Fair Choice
2538	Need A Helping Hand With Your New Business
2539	I'll Give You The Keys To My Malibu Mansion
2540	How's Your About Page
2541	All In A Single Stroke
2542	If You Create It
2543	See How Crazy It Gets
2544	How To Make Salesletters Interactive
2545	Why Keep Going Down Blind Marketing Alleys
2546	Stop Messing Around With Losers
2547	There Are Words That Will Keep You Poor
2548	Here Are Some Of The Great Things You'll Enjoy
2549	We Want To Hear The Story
2550	This Will Change Your Life Forever
2551	Look For Pain Plus Urgency
2552	Accomplish More In Less Time
2553	Choose A Niche Within A Niche
2554	Why Social Media Isn't A Career
2555	Zero Results Never Again
2556	Making Money Guide To Real Wealth
2557	Flexible Perks
2558	The Key Is - Not On Their Own
2559	This Is Something You Should Not Miss

2560	It Sounds Like A Smart Move
2561	Want Massive Traffic
2562	Hidden Impact
2563	Those Shiny Object Just Drain Money
2564	Solid Home Business
2565	Every Internet Marketer Needs This System
2566	Rant And Rave
2567	What Are You Going To Be
2568	You'll Want To Catch This
2569	Speak Your Message
2570	Trial Offers Are Extremely Scalable
2571	Celebrity Is The New Currency
2572	Really Big Mistake
2573	Point Your Browser To...
2574	Includes Video For Higher Conversions
2575	Foolish To Close This Door
2576	Minimum And Maximum Price Ranges
2577	It's Time To Break The Impasse
2578	No Cancellation Fees
2579	Start With Nothing And Publish
2580	Two Tools I Always Use
2581	A Well Oiled Money-Making Machine
2582	Appropriate Pricing Strategy
2583	From Drab To Fab
2584	Did You Fall For This
2585	Your Dreams Realized
2586	What Now
2587	Create Cliffhanger To Seal The Deal
2588	Avoiding The Humiliation Of Rejection
2589	Building Ultra Responsive Lists
2590	Invest In Your Brain
2591	Your Read It Correctly You Keep All The Commissions
2592	Are Your Values Expanding Your Potential
2593	I'm Not Charging A Penny For This
2594	Tap Into Their Wonder
2595	Add Fun To Life
2596	These Transactions Can Dramatically Benefit You
2597	Find A Market With A High Ticket Product

81

2598	Who Uses Mail Anymore
2599	What's Your Unique Benefit
2600	Pulling Buyers In From All Directions
2601	We Have Work To Do
2602	Losing A Great Deal Or Getting It
2603	Why They End Up Pulped
2604	There's A Problem
2605	Let Me Join Your Team
2606	Long Form Sales Copy That Makes Money
2607	Reducing Your Power
2608	I Quit Using Adwords Forever
2609	Learn This Trick For Yourself
2610	The Best Framework Ever Discovered To Teach Others
2611	You Learn A Lot About Your Business With This Conversation
2612	Get Adventures Out Of A Smile
2613	Clickbank Calculator Software
2614	This Is Where High I.Q. People Fail
2615	Time To Upgrade Your Life
2616	Access The World Of Source
2617	Death Of Yellow Pages
2618	You Can Cancel Whenever You Want
2619	Flair And Classy Clothes
2620	Most Powerful Opt-In System Ever Created
2621	Ideas That Die Well
2622	Popularity Focused
2623	This Becomes Exceptionally Helpful
2624	Start Research Curious Background Stories
2625	Never Turn Back
2626	Your Million Dollar Rolodex
2627	Sit Back And Watch The Money Flood In
2628	I Agree One Hundred Percent
2629	Building Block Solutions
2630	It's Not Always About Working Hard
2631	Sell Your People First
2632	Everything You Really Need To Know
2633	Register Early
2634	You'll Never Ever Have To Pay For Advertising Again
2635	A Great Headline Can Be Worth Millions

2636	Your First Cash Register
2637	Don't Just Become A Spare Part
2638	Warning This Information Will Change Your Thoughts
2639	Right Now Is The Crucial Moment To Decide
2640	Have You Ever Had Someone Like This In Your Life
2641	How To Zip
2642	No More Struggling
2643	Audio Books
2644	Leverage Their Mentality
2645	New Hope For Struggling Marketers
2646	Guaranteed To Fill Over And Over
2647	Can You Handle Having Power Over Others
2648	Do You Need A Revolutionary Idea To Bring To Market
2649	How To Achieve Reality
2650	Personal Strategies, Habits And Secret Tools
2651	Adwords Scheduling
2652	Create An Amazon Two Pizza Team
2653	Multiply Your Profits
2654	Notice Some Honest Marketers
2655	When Do You Need It
2656	Order Now, Pay Later
2657	Spreading Cell To Cell
2658	Hire Professional To Do That
2659	You're Invited On My Next Cruise
2660	Going Off The Grid
2661	Succeed As A Consultant
2662	No More Just Looking Responses
2663	Willing To Really Start Today
2664	We Grow Money Not Hair
2665	Escaping The impending Rat Race
2666	You Won't Pay $997
2667	Laughing Too Little
2668	Doesn't Have To Be Difficult
2669	Conflict Resolved
2670	Why Most Experts Only Have A Job
2671	Sustain Your Voice Longer
2672	Start Using These Headlines In Your Business Now
2673	How About A Double Dose Of Secret Shattering Tips

2674	Here's The Basic Idea
2675	Convert Visitors Into Subscribers!
2676	Doesn't It All Seem Undaunting
2677	I Did It The Unselfish Way
2678	Perhaps I'm Getting Ahead Of Myself
2679	Instant Solutions To Frequently Asked Questions
2680	Impact Of Random Events
2681	Black Friday II
2682	Police Your Own Money
2683	A Name For Your Product
2684	Move It Into The Cloud
2685	Hit Different Triggers
2686	Satisfy Curiosity
2687	It's Just Too Easy
2688	Will The Internet Replace Your TV
2689	Snockered And Unstable
2690	Tricks And Techniques For Skyrocketing Profits
2691	Visual One Page Project
2692	Bad Boy Busted
2693	Enormous Swings
2694	Experimentation Is Key To Innovation
2695	Create Bigger Paychecks Fast
2696	Your New Partner Does Want You To Succeed
2697	That's Also The Upside
2698	How To Make Money Even When You Fell Rotten
2699	Marketing Pain Shouldn't Get In Your Way
2700	Tools Designed For Me
2701	Did You Really Miss This
2702	Imagine The Potential Sales
2703	Shortcut Secrets
2704	Life Without Limits
2705	The Central Figure
2706	Partly Conscious Approach
2707	The More Focused The More Success
2708	The Average Hospital Bill Has $600 In Phony Charges.
2709	Your Personal Stimulus Plan
2710	Something Big Is On The Way
2711	The Tweeter Generation

2712	Activate Your Holiday Mojo
2713	What Every Entrepreneur Fears
2714	Seeking A Joint Venture
2715	Managing Your Money
2716	3 Ways To Seal The Deal
2717	Why Love Them Then Leave Them
2718	For Those Who Seek Instant Motivation
2719	Physical vs. Mental Snacking
2720	This Amazing Technique Can Fool 9 out of 10 Experts
2721	Direct Bank Deposits Make Marketing Easier
2722	Power Up Your Surf Center Now
2723	Get Paid To Have A Blast
2724	Are They Scaring You To Death
2725	Looking For Partners
2726	Looking For Professionals
2727	Is Your Unprofitable Site Embarrassing
2728	The Mini Documentary
2729	Find The Perfect Offer
2730	Making Eye Contact With The Camera
2731	Just Follow The Money
2732	The Joy Of You
2733	Still Wasting Your Marketing Shots
2734	Drag The Viewer Right In
2735	Still Time To Cut Your Taxes
2736	Why Men With Visions Go Broke
2737	The Cornerstones Of Our Life
2738	Scratch Your Niche
2739	Some People Just Need A Real Person's Help
2740	It's Slipping Away As We Speak
2741	It Plays Just Like A Movie
2742	Our Products Speak For Themselves
2743	It's All In The Rollups
2744	Get A Grip On These Tips
2745	The Problem And Why It's Happening
2746	Mountain Top Adss New Traffic Exchange
2747	Will They Want To Know The Answer
2748	It's Going Nutso Around Here
2749	In Brief

2750	Create A Lasting Brand For Yourself Online
2751	Free Traffic
2752	Just How Powerful Is This
2753	What To Do With Your Subscribers
2754	Master Information
2755	Simple Research That Brings You Wealth
2756	The Most Profitable For You
2757	Online Meetings Made Easy
2758	Lot Of Tools And Resources
2759	In The Spiral Of Things Getting Worse
2760	Does Your Mic Rustle When You Talk
2761	Just When You Thought All The Good Ideas Were Taken
2762	Ever Wanted To Buy It All
2763	They're Not Laughing After I Made My First Dollar
2764	Sales Letters Are Not Dead
2765	Writing The Rules
2766	Alleviate Stress In All Your Customers
2767	Manage Any Size Network
2768	Get This Rebrandable eBook Now
2769	Analyze Your List Carefully For Flaws
2770	Marketing Eyeball Assault
2771	10 Eye Popping, Jaw Dropping Ad Copy Secrets
2772	Video Search Engine Optimization
2773	Legal Espionage
2774	Are The Rumors True
2775	Startling News Flash
2776	The Only Stupid Question Is The One Never Asked
2777	The Best Short Cut You'll Ever Find
2778	Why They Just Tune Out
2779	Web Tool Development
2780	Release Your Limitations
2781	Now Is The Time To Learn
2782	I Know You're So Rich You Don't Need This
2783	Don't Know About PLR
2784	Set It Up And Walk Away
2785	Free Crystal Ball That Tells All
2786	Spillover Profits
2787	Use Buttons And Links To Test Your Order Now Links

2788	Why Some Businesses Survive And Thrive In Hard Times
2789	Why Should I Take A Closer Look
2790	Right Help At The Right Time
2791	Her Crazy Sense Of Humor
2792	Green Is The New Gold
2793	Embed These Into Your Headlines
2794	Why Did They Say NO
2795	Need Some Time For Yourself
2796	How To Only Invest Time Not Money
2797	All You Really Need Is One Simple Idea
2798	Super Goal Setting Secrets
2799	Simplest Steps People Use To Succeed
2800	Pick Up A Free Sample
2801	The Power Behind Expectation
2802	The First Thing You Need To Know
2803	Step Into Nature
2804	Why Must You Win
2805	No Roadblocks Or Barriers To Enter
2806	They All Skim Around Your Offer
2807	Last Minute Bonus
2808	I'll Walk You Through This Exercise
2809	Yeah I Really Do It Myself
2810	Start Out With Quality
2811	Make Money Playing Online Poker
2812	There's No Hook
2813	Hang On Because It Just Gets Better And Better
2814	What If I Offered You Something Unique
2815	It Shows Me Where To Go
2816	What's The Catch - There Is None
2817	Quit Challenging Everything And Just Do It
2818	Move The World With A Longer Leverage
2819	Power Of The Past
2820	Now You Too Can Kiss Your Internet Worries Goodbye Forever
2821	Join Our Winning Team
2822	I'm Not Going To Oversell This
2823	Do Just The Opposite And You'll Succeed
2824	Combining The Right Mindset
2825	Break It Down - Making It Simple

2826	There's No Faster Way To Grow
2827	Maybe You'll See What I Saw
2828	Clickbank Vendor Cloaking Secrets
2829	White Label Products
2830	Don't Wait For Something To Happen
2831	Avoid Wanting A Bigger Vision For Yourself
2832	Let's Fix The Problem
2833	This School Is In The Clouds
2834	Double Down
2835	I Became An Internet Marketing Sponge
2836	It's A Must
2837	Stop Refunders And File Sharers
2838	Your Humanity Makes You Relatable
2839	Entertainment At A Great Price
2840	Select High Profile Partners
2841	The Greatest Online Navigator Will Steer You Toward New Horizons
2842	Prove Your Worth
2843	Compile A 100 Day Ecourse
2844	How Prepared Are You
2845	Tantamount Terror
2846	Oh Yah Money Money Money
2847	Stealing Your Money
2848	Bargain Basement Bonanza
2849	No Previous Experience Required
2850	Send The Traffic To You First
2851	Look At What You Get For Free
2852	Clarity Supported By Action
2853	Don't Know Where To Start
2854	How Can We Add Another Product To Our Menu
2855	Extraordinary Residual Income
2856	Is The Life Of A Child Worth $1 To You
2857	Sense Of Urgency
2858	Don't Be Transparent Be Authentic Instead
2859	Gaining Global Clout
2860	No Swiping Allowed
2861	Because I Know My Stuff Is Good
2862	Don't Allow Your Inner Critic To Censor Your Ideas
2863	Full Details In Seconds

2864	Access Opportunities When Listening To Customers
2865	Who Do I Know That Can Solve Your Problem
2866	Chalk One Up
2867	Stages Of Buyer Awareness
2868	Our Goals Are Pretty Simple
2869	Recipe For Disaster
2870	Does Your Business Still Struggle With A Negative Bank Account
2871	When Shipping And Handling Pays For All Of It
2872	Inspire And Engage Your Sales Team
2873	Host Your Site Online Within A Collaborative Environment
2874	Hypnosis Vs. Computer Games
2875	Can You Keep A Secret
2876	Free Comprehensive Survey Allows You To...
2877	Want To Work With Like-Minded Marketers
2878	Think I'm On To Something BIG
2879	Start A Profitable Membership Site
2880	Traffic Success Solution
2881	How Much Pain Do You Require
2882	Would This Totally Change Everything
2883	Limited By DeFacto Standard Marketing Practices
2884	All The Matters Is What Your Customers Need
2885	When Your Image Isn't Working
2886	Cashing Out After Cashing In
2887	How To Protect Your Online Business
2888	Focus On Developing These Tips Not Tricks To Become Success-ful
2889	Sloppy Thinking Equals Loss
2890	Refine Your Marketing Sonar
2891	Works Beyond Expectations
2892	Home Business Opportunities
2893	Pad Your Wallet
2894	A Product that Pays Residual Income
2895	See And Touch Your Target
2896	Confidence Worth Observing
2897	Freedom From Daily Problems
2898	You Know You Can Become A Teacher
2899	Everybody's Got Their Niche
2900	Online Training Is Exploding
2901	Throwing It Together Quickly Produces Junk

2902	Build Income Not Just A Business
2903	Start Early And Live Long
2904	Pull The Trigger Now
2905	Buying Businesses Simplified
2906	Start Banking Your Profits
2907	Promote Monthly During The Last Week
2908	Seeking A Serious Collaborative Effort
2909	How To Handle Life's Frustration
2910	Every Hero Has A Downfall
2911	Looking For That Special Boss
2912	Gardening Is My Graffiti When I Grow My Own Art
2913	Enjoy Life While Doing The Right Thing
2914	Stoking Your Own Fires
2915	Make Your Point Stick
2916	Undisputable Champions
2917	You're Faced With THREE BIG PROBLEMS
2918	How To Win The War Of Internet Marketing
2919	Success Is The Fruit Of Learning
2920	Failure Due To Bad Design
2921	Holy Fakes
2922	Dreamweaver Squeeze Video Settings
2923	Master Customization Rights
2924	Watering Yourself Down
2925	Before I Get Started
2926	Looped And Duped
2927	Pull An All-Nighter
2928	You Need To Know This Information
2929	Making Tough Decisions
2930	Cyber Competition
2931	It's Official
2932	Tuck It Behind Your Ear
2933	Your Download Is Free
2934	So Damn Obvious
2935	Why People End Up With Your Money
2936	Ad Must Get Their Point Across
2937	Fine Tune The Quality Of Your Business Innovations
2938	Avoid Looking Down
2939	Blog Set Up Themes

90

2940	Want A Business That Makes Money
2941	Earn On The Internet
2942	Nothing's Going To Stop You Now
2943	What Do You Need In Order To Achieve That Result
2944	Brand Names Use To Mean Better
2945	Identify Profitable Topics Within Your Niche
2946	Without Buyers A Business Dies
2947	Taking Steps To Close The Gap
2948	Has Your Mail Server Been Blacklisted
2949	Continual Battle To Keep Subscribers
2950	Snatch This Up
2951	I Want To Find Out More About You
2952	What's Expected Of You
2953	Are You Prepared To Be Wrong
2954	Make Contact With Your Audience
2955	Do You Want To Go All Out
2956	You're Getting A 30-Day FREE Membership
2957	Doable For Anyone
2958	How To Extract The Data
2959	What's The Steepest Goal You've Set
2960	Deep Breathing And Meditation
2961	Don't These Drive You Crazy
2962	Speed Up Your Income
2963	Accentuate Your Features
2964	So Why Are You Doing It
2965	Big Decisions Deserve Thorough Due Diligence
2966	Turn On The Fire House Of Submissions
2967	You Can Wish All You Want
2968	Recording The Path To Freedom
2969	Back To School
2970	Let Me Tell You A Story
2971	Growing Faster Than A Wildfire
2972	For Quick Information Call...
2973	How To Choose The Best Program For Max Profits
2974	Based Upon What Best Fits Your Needs
2975	Please Stop The Frustration
2976	Be Just As Proud
2977	Take Immediate Action

2978	Reduce Frictional Unemployment And Save Money
2979	This System Will Never Saturate The Market
2980	Increase Your Search Visibility
2981	Give Yourself An Instant Pay Raise
2982	Stop Being Tossed In The Trash
2983	Become A Business Wizard And Pave Your Way To Success
2984	An Impressive Ear Piece
2985	Start Down Your Own Road
2986	Free Instant eBook Download
2987	Where Are You Right Now Really
2988	Propelled By Rhythm
2989	Look For The HOT Bonus Inside
2990	Amazing Offer Sets Marketing On Fire
2991	Relentless Marketing Will Expose An Urban Myth About Money
2992	Maybe The Truth Is Not What You Want To Hear
2993	Taylor Made For You
2994	Don't Just Hand Out Your Business Cards
2995	Dealing With Abstract Marketing Ideas
2996	Keep Your Headlines Sans Serif Font
2997	Network Like A Pro
2998	Are You One That Makes Things Happen
2999	Wish I Had Written That
3000	Put This In Your Sleigh
3001	7 Reasons Why You Must Start Your Own Business TODAY
3002	Best of The Michel Fortin Blog in 2008
3003	Stealing Ideas From Nature
3004	Weather Is A Mood, Climate Is A Personality
3005	Create Your Own Products
3006	The Art Of Marketing Mind Control
3007	Embrace The Contrast
3008	Fair Warning - We May Remove It At Any Time
3009	They're Just Trying To Get Your Attention
3010	How To Automate Your Online Business
3011	Getting An Emotional Fix
3012	How To Get And Register A Google Email Account
3013	Expand Your Bank Vault With This Bottom Line Approach
3014	You Can Never Have Enough Sub Headlines
3015	How To Fail Giving Away Free Money

3016	Develop Your Profit Instincts
3017	Provide It Different Ways
3018	When You Go Paperless
3019	Free Shocking Video
3020	Wanna Work For Me
3021	How Do You DO IT With Words
3022	Automated Business Builder
3023	New Summer Scandals
3024	We Only Act In The NOW
3025	Desire Leads To Action
3026	Must Have Certain Set Of Skills
3027	Act Now To Learn More
3028	What Are You Working On
3029	Qualities Tougher To Quantify
3030	Create The Highest Caliber B3B Cast Ever Assembled
3031	Adding To The Economic Pie
3032	Earn Extra Marketing Credit Points
3033	In Only 30 Minutes
3034	Customers Proven To Buy
3035	Commission Thieves Are A Very Real Threat
3036	The Work Is Well Worth It
3037	Suspicious Activity Reports
3038	We Got Sick Of The Daily Grind
3039	Take Your Time But Hurry
3040	Your I.M. Retirement Plan
3041	The Brain Is Built To Respond
3042	Mini-Course With An Attention Grabbing Name
3043	Are Mp3s Illegal
3044	Informative And Straight To The Point
3045	Enable And Inspire
3046	Communicate And Lead Through Powerful Stories
3047	Exactly Who Are You Trying To Reach
3048	Zig Zagging Doesn't Lead To Happiness
3049	Think Long Term
3050	When Times Are Good
3051	What Does A Millionaire Look Like
3052	Real World Traffic
3053	The Moment Of My Big Breakthrough

93

3054	A Revolutionary Program Providing Unlimited Possibilities
3055	Prove The Naysayer Dead Wrong
3056	Let's Get Moving
3057	Failure Is Not Forever
3058	Engage Them Within 3 Seconds
3059	Execution Strategies That Produce Huge Profits
3060	When You're Grown Up
3061	Automate Your Payday
3062	It's About The Life You Want
3063	Your Video Showcase
3064	Free Trial Offer
3065	Hot Weekly Deals
3066	Cold Hard Truths
3067	The Safelist Directory Ebook
3068	Hardcore Proof From An Affiliate Master
3069	Generate All The Referrals You'll Ever Need
3070	Win Money Online
3071	Maven Of Your Market Niche
3072	Savvy Street Smart Lessons
3073	Fundamental Actions You Need To Take Right Now
3074	The Highest Impact Categories
3075	Take A Vacation Whenever You Want
3076	Ready For Whirlwind Exposure
3077	High Quality
3078	Does Your Bosshole Act Like He's Doing You A Favor
3079	Think Extensively Not Intensively
3080	Start Stacking Your Dollars
3081	Maintaining A High Variety Of Content
3082	Advertise Just About Any Product Or Service
3083	Your Opportunity To Set The Price
3084	Quick Cash Certificates
3085	Blast Those Roadblocks Away
3086	How Did They Find This
3087	Just For Your
3088	Get Star Treatment
3089	Is Your Site Under-Performing
3090	Changing Friends Faster Than Underwear
3091	Advertiser Offers Humongous FREE Ad Space

3092	What Is It That You Do Exactly
3093	Incredible Energetic And Positive Responses
3094	No Time No Energy
3095	Prying Identity Theft
3096	It's Vitally Important
3097	Research For Effective Article Writing
3098	We Are Here To Push You Forward
3099	What Do You Do Just For Fun
3100	Get The Right Ideas In Your Head
3101	For All Your Girlfriends
3102	When Value Is Clear Decisions Are Easy
3103	Arresting Sales Slumps
3104	Follow Up On A Regular Basis
3105	Scare Yourself Into Bettering Yourself Fast
3106	All Aren't Dogs Equal Woof Woof
3107	Practices That Threaten Survival
3108	Tweak And Refine
3109	Face Your Fears
3110	My Push Button Empire Wants You
3111	Joint Venture Investor
3112	Go Ahead Drop Your Blog On Me
3113	Viable Balance
3114	Free Landing Page
3115	You'll Find This Is Actually More Than A Little Misleading
3116	Adopting Creative Thinking
3117	Too Busy Doing It Wrong
3118	Why We Want You To Be Rich
3119	Are You Wasting Your Time Creating False Value
3120	Do The Right Thing Online And Reap Incredible Rewards
3121	But Wait There's More
3122	Success And Family Aren't Incompatible
3123	Industry Leading 100% Money Back Guarantee
3124	They Have No Clue Who's Behind It
3125	Changing Consumer Habits
3126	My Hard-Earned Secrets
3127	Be In Control Of Your Own Destiny
3128	Now Being Allocated
3129	Where Your Prospects Are

3130	On The Road To Success
3131	Want To Wiggle More Orders Your Way
3132	Start Banking Profits Immediately
3133	Discover The Coolness Inside
3134	Become Conscious Of Facial Expressions
3135	Need An Estimate
3136	There Really Is No Downside
3137	Need An Occasional Kick In The Butt
3138	Create An Order-Pulling Niche
3139	Gallons Of Sweat
3140	Pamper Your Marketing Problem Away
3141	Before Your Feet Hit The Ground
3142	9 Out Of 10 People Have Never Read An eBook
3143	A Better Way To Steal Traffic
3144	Still Listening To What Others Think You Can't Do
3145	Make Your Computer Impenetrable
3146	Here's Your Shiny New Password
3147	Direct From The Marketing World
3148	Worth Your While Looking
3149	Do You Still Have Something To Prove
3150	The Truth vs. The Real Truth
3151	Why Multilingual Sites Make More Money
3152	Like An Easter Egg Hunt
3153	Affiliate Commerce Frenzy
3154	Unlimited Number Of Ideas
3155	This Is How It Works
3156	How Much Should I Charge For This Content
3157	Work Directly With Out-Sourced Workers
3158	Piggyback On Free Traffic
3159	You'll Want To Do This Today
3160	Special Period Of Excellent Opportunity
3161	We Too Take Part
3162	Stop Being An Entrepreneur
3163	Reap The Real Rewards Online
3164	You Need To Read This Page Now Because…
3165	Find Your Alone Time
3166	Focusing On Results
3167	Penalty Flags To Watch For

3168	Does This Piece Resonant
3169	For Under Performing Products
3170	Subscribers Are Racking Up Big Time Commission Checks
3171	Calling All Property Owners
3172	Some Think I Must Be Crazy
3173	Essential Autoresponder Tips
3174	I'm Gonna Take Advantage Of Your Temporary Insanity
3175	Enter The Headline Spectacularity Zone
3176	Marketing Receiver
3177	Reinforce Beneficial Solutions
3178	Thou Shall Find More With Less
3179	Ready To Buy
3180	My Life Had Purpose Again
3181	Business Goldmine
3182	Offline Consulting Step By Step
3183	Win The Jackpot
3184	That Someone Can Be You
3185	I Just Can't Tell Everyone
3186	A Free Ticket To My Telecast
3187	Create Your Own Personal Ad System
3188	Just Be You
3189	Driven By Irrational Passion
3190	Online Presentation LIVE Tomorrow
3191	And I Thought They Wanted My Business
3192	Only $7 To Start A Business - Yes
3193	Money-Back-Plus Guarantee
3194	Powerful Self-Help Program
3195	This Tactic Could Make Or Break You
3196	Pick Your Plan Now
3197	Find Out Who's Talking
3198	The Monthly Pay Model
3199	I Just Love Giving Money Away
3200	Scale Plus Automation
3201	How To Create Your Own Lead Pulling Squeeze Page
3202	Distract Yourself
3203	How Well Do You Manage Risk
3204	Transferable Master Resale Rights
3205	Video Streaming

3206	Redesign Your Life
3207	Those With A Plan Or Those With Money
3208	Our Lives Are Entangled
3209	Does Your Business Overlook This Glaring Hole
3210	Incredible Graphic Designs
3211	I'm Living Proof This System Works
3212	Turn Up Your Speakers And Watch This Video Right Now
3213	How To Find A Properly Focused Action Plan
3214	Last Seat Being Jerked Out Under You
3215	Start Off With A Couple Of Short Stories
3216	Most Frustrating Part About Starting An Online Business
3217	True Or False You Have No Worries
3218	My Advice - Go There Now
3219	One Great Price
3220	Cantankerous Customers
3221	Keep It Under 3 Minutes
3222	This Requires Imagination
3223	Organize Life On Your Terms
3224	Make More Money Invisibly
3225	The Most Valuable Asset On Earth
3226	Master Abilities That Can't Be Outsourced
3227	Using Bold Print Or Underlines
3228	We'll Bill You Later
3229	How To Turn Your Business Around Virtually Overnight
3230	Milking Monday Meetings
3231	Why Our Members Learn More While Making More Money
3232	What's A One Percenter
3233	Free Video Blog Series
3234	Why Drip Feeding Is More Effective
3235	Proven Spectacularly Profitable
3236	Here's What You'll Discover Before Anyone Else
3237	No Cheesy One Time Deals Here
3238	It's Not What You Do - It's How You Do It
3239	Inventing New Reasons For Failure
3240	Track Links To External Sites And Services
3241	No Experience Necessary
3242	Want To Listen Without Reading The PDF
3243	Long Hours And Still Nothing To Show

3244	No Longer Just Part Of The Herd
3245	This Manual Provides A Fresh Start
3246	Too Many Jokers Online
3247	Today's Gonna Be Fun
3248	Focus On Building Great Opt-In Lists
3249	Social Search Is Shifting
3250	It Isn't Only Luck Anymore
3251	Even In Darker Times
3252	Don't Let My Insanity Turn You On
3253	Live Your Message
3254	How To Implement The Perfect Backend Strategy
3255	Get In Front Of The Camera Everyday
3256	Get Incredible FREE Research About Hot Offers... Right Now!
3257	The Secret To Unleashing Your Genius
3258	How These Cannibalize Sales
3259	Hold A Free Teleseminar
3260	Marketing Incursions
3261	What Are You Missing
3262	When Diseases Weren't Yet Invented
3263	Earn A Deeper Level Of Trust
3264	Refer People To Membership Sites
3265	Delve Deep Into This Niche
3266	The Most Important Technique Ever Known To Mankind
3267	Give Them Less Incentive To Steal
3268	The Format Is Simple
3269	New 60 Page Guide
3270	There Will Be More Pain
3271	One On One
3272	You Don't Even Need A Website
3273	From The Vault
3274	America's Foremost Millionaire
3275	Beyond Keywords
3276	Check This Box For Your Bonus
3277	This Book Is Really That Powerful
3278	It Just Got A Whole Lot Better
3279	Stop Begging
3280	Secrets You'll Never Learn From Anyone Else
3281	Trouble Converting

3282	If You Only Do It Once
3283	Looking For A Lucrative Compensation Plan
3284	Stop Them From Stealing Your Products
3285	Blast Your Site To Uncharted Heights
3286	You're Not Coming Down Slowly
3287	Who, What, When, Where, and Why
3288	Purchases Start With Trust
3289	I'll Cut Out The Suspense
3290	On A Rampage Of Appreciation
3291	Questionable Damage
3292	Don't Play Marketing Games With Customers
3293	Sunny Sunday Saver
3294	Cycle Through Everything You Know
3295	Don't Miss This Wonderful Opportunity
3296	We Have Some Presents For You
3297	Free Upon Request
3298	Stay Grounded Into Your Body
3299	Ditch The Quilt
3300	A Video Without A Video Camera Or Microphone
3301	Raising Your Energy Levels
3302	Pick Up A Marketing Hobby
3303	Put Audio Ads On Your Website
3304	Sharing Similar Frames Of Reference
3305	New Products Pop Up Each Day
3306	Let Me Be Brutally Blunt
3307	Your Service Provider Doesn't Know Jack
3308	The Breathing Space You Need
3309	The More Specific The Better
3310	Can't Afford It
3311	Duplication Of Successful Marketing Efforts
3312	Maybe This Is Suppose To Happen
3313	What Happens At The End Of The Day
3314	Profit Guide Full Of Tips Tricks And Tactics
3315	More Sales For The Same Effort
3316	Are They Biting On You Niche
3317	Out Of Ideas
3318	The Different Parameters Of Success
3319	Find Your Comfort Zone

3320	How Can You Possibly Go Back The Old Way
3321	Every Imaginable Niche Has A Market
3322	I Found You A New Job
3323	After 9 Months It's Finally Born
3324	It's Hard To Walk And Chew Gum
3325	Dogs Need A Knowledgeable Trainer And So Do People
3326	All Work Is Run By Technology
3327	Winners Emerge
3328	Move Forward With Confidence
3329	Knowing Where You've Been
3330	Your Brand Disappearing Without A Trace
3331	Finally Someone Is Blasting These Wannabe Scams
3332	Pay $7 One Time
3333	Marketing Disaster Has Created Huge Opportunities
3334	Stop Fretting Over Pennies
3335	Predictable Scalable And Consistent
3336	Is This Your Missing Link
3337	Direct Result Of Tiny Simple Changes
3338	Before You Open Up
3339	Do You Use It
3340	Afraid To Answer The Phone
3341	Who Is The Decision Maker
3342	Turn Your Points Into Cash Money
3343	Got A Phone Pencil And Pad Of Paper
3344	People Will Eventually Get It
3345	At A Price Anyone Can Afford
3346	An Accomplished Liar
3347	Action Required
3348	Best Freebie In The World
3349	Normal Means Mediocre
3350	Speak With Passion
3351	Entering Negative Territory
3352	I Get It Now
3353	Why Work So Hard For Something You'll Never Own
3354	Cash Back Without Thinking
3355	Sure Fire Profit Plans
3356	The Hub Of Creative Thoughts
3357	All About Giving Value

3358	The Actions That Create The Money
3359	The Next Step Was
3360	My Bottom Line
3361	A Few Hours Per Week Of Your Time
3362	Commit To Your Vision
3363	World's Greatest Response
3364	The Secret Is Out
3365	Want To Fill Your Piggy Bank
3366	They're All Free Once You Come Inside
3367	Offer Yourself The Gift Of Success
3368	You Have To Know How This Feels
3369	Your Best Weapon For Success
3370	I Don't Mind
3371	Hosting Secrets Revealed
3372	Simplicity Rules In Copy Writing
3373	Get A Good Night's Sleep
3374	Deathwatch Of The Gold Watch And 40-Year Pension
3375	I'll Be Quick
3376	Fall Into Wisconsin
3377	Has Theirs Ever Made You Money
3378	2 Second Page Loads
3379	Flow Of Energy Flows To Action
3380	Freeze Your Money By Not Wasting It On These Mistakes
3381	Avoid Fashion Logos On Videos
3382	A Crisis Can Erupt At Any Moment
3383	Will eReaders Become A Necessity
3384	Instantly Profit From Subscribers
3385	Quit Being A Lab Rat
3386	Overlooking Simple Solutions
3387	Minnows vs. Whales Marketing
3388	Two Possible Fates
3389	Do You Have An Ask Campaign
3390	Simple & Practical
3391	Find 10 Emotional Niches
3392	Understanding Client's Wants And Needs
3393	One Succinct Paragraph
3394	Becoming Your Message
3395	Original Profound And Amazingly Thought Provoking

3396	It's Never One Size Fits All In This Market
3397	Are You Ready To Roar
3398	Need Answers Fast
3399	You'll Get Everything You Need To Customize This
3400	The Big Lie
3401	Jump In While The Water Is Still Warm
3402	Become Transparent And Real
3403	It's Not Easy At First
3404	Future Weapons
3405	For Those Who Don't Like To Read
3406	What You Believe Can Limit Your Success
3407	It's LIVE Go Go Go
3408	Your Life's Dreams Lie Just Ahead
3409	Internet Marketing Can Be Hard
3410	You Know What They Want
3411	Eyes Are The Mirrors To Your Soul
3412	Zero Risk Looking And Listening
3413	Being Secure Has Nothing To Do With Your Job
3414	Dust It Off
3415	See What I Just Developed
3416	Take Control Of Your Customers
3417	An Emotional Connection With Another Human Being
3418	Bottom Up Preference
3419	They Will Pay You With Their Time
3420	Do Your Header Graphics Suck
3421	How Self-Deceit Ultimately Destroys Success
3422	Seize The Moment
3423	Only $10 More And You Get Them Both
3424	At Absolutely No Cost To You
3425	The Best Damn Dollar I Ever Spent
3426	Timely Action Is Required Now
3427	Keep A Consistent Conversational Tone
3428	Looking Forward To The New One
3429	Why Successful Businesses Focus On What's In It For Them
3430	Need High Quality Resources
3431	Monetization Tip To Make High Commissions
3432	Build The Muscle Skill And Habit
3433	Internet Money-Maker Madness Is Here

3434	Flood Your PP Account With Payments
3435	Eliminate All The Guess Work
3436	Start Leading The Way
3437	Just The Facts
3438	Sick And Tired Of The Drudgery
3439	Please Check Your Email For The Information You Requested
3440	Edit Two Files
3441	Who Else Wants To Earn Money & Respect
3442	Click Here To Apply
3443	No Advertising Budget - No Problem
3444	Take A Look At These Screen Shots
3445	Don't Take Retirement Sitting Down
3446	Turn On Even The Most Disinterested Prospects
3447	Becoming A Seasoned Pro Without The Missteps
3448	You Have To Be Strong
3449	A Confused Mind Never Buys
3450	You Already Have A Specialty
3451	Sunggle Under Your Technology Blanket
3452	Don't Let Them Pull The Wool Over Your Eyes
3453	The Perfect Combination
3454	On Fire With New Bonuses
3455	Writing A Book Will Change Your Life
3456	Don't Become A Slave To Your Computer
3457	But You Already Knew That
3458	Create Good Backgrounds
3459	Give People Options
3460	Still Jumping Through Marketing Hoops
3461	Is This Too Good To Be True
3462	Connection And Inspiration
3463	How To Upsell With Extended Benefits
3464	Thousands Have This Priceless Gift But Never Discover It
3465	A Job Is Only 2 Paychecks From Disaster
3466	The Barrier To Feeling Successful
3467	My Gamble Finally Paid Off
3468	Task Bar Raises Glass To Success
3469	Push The Boundaries To Explore Its Profit
3470	There's Nothing Wrong With Wanting More
3471	Life Requires Asking

3472	Blogospheres Have Evolved Into Money-Making Machines
3473	Clean The Stupid Out Of Their Ears And Listen Up
3474	Before They Lost Their Way
3475	These Will Sell Out Fast
3476	Feed Yourself Figuratively
3477	Are You Hearing I Want What You Have
3478	Listen Up
3479	How To Have What You Want
3480	Digging Down Deep
3481	We're Not That Different
3482	Generate Keyword Lists
3483	Only 10 Percent Of The Additional Revenue Brought In
3484	Take Happiness Seriously
3485	Do You Know Who's Following You
3486	I Re-Doubled My Efforts
3487	Hit Record And Start Talking
3488	This Is Who I Am
3489	Giving Yourself A Raise Without Asking Your Boss
3490	You Can Enroll Now
3491	Take Just One Piece And Experience Success
3492	Okay Where Is The Catch
3493	Blue Prints For Success Are Always Built Upon A System
3494	Overcome Obstacles
3495	Occupied My Thoughts Every Hour Of The Day
3496	Work At Your Leisure
3497	Easiest Way To Customize Your Own Site
3498	A Serendipitous Way To Start
3499	Five In One Products
3500	Self-Stamped Envelope That Brings Results
3501	Refining Sell
3502	Master The Basics
3503	Valued Command Chain Locks In Profits
3504	Only 24 Hours Left
3505	By Joining Today You'll Receive
3506	More Customers Will Buy Your Product
3507	Never Have To Work Another Day Again
3508	Access Real World Promotions
3509	Wishing You Happiness Joy And Laughter

3510	Get On With It
3511	The Following Pages Will Make You Rich
3512	You'll Make Changes In Your Business After Reading This
3513	Does That Sound Good To You
3514	Value Equals Response
3515	Feeling Locked Out Of The Money Game
3516	Transform Sad Feelings Instantly
3517	Tune Into Source Energy
3518	Test Your Niche
3519	How Cool Is It Going To Work Now
3520	Make Lots Of Money With This Little Secret
3521	You're About To Create History
3522	Are You A Millionaire Copywriter
3523	I'm Ready To Leave My Competition In The Dust
3524	Want To Partner With Incredible Tools Products And Services
3525	If You Could Pick Just One
3526	Learn Why It's Not Your Fault
3527	Gain Big Skills Fast
3528	Progress Limiting Phenomenon
3529	Almost *Force* People To Hand You Thick Wads Of Cash
3530	Super Charge The Process
3531	The Newest Cutting Edge Secrets Revealed Here
3532	This Program's Free
3533	Content Is The Lifeblood Of Our Business
3534	Backend Coaching
3535	Why Marketing Is Afraid Of The Truth
3536	Becoming A Gum Shoe
3537	Lion Or Lioness
3538	This Will Enable You To
3539	I'm The Only One Allowed To Promote This Product
3540	What Would It Look Like If It Was Perfect
3541	Incredible First Paragraph
3542	A Book Filled With Magic Bullets
3543	Launching Your Own Affiliate Program
3544	This Is An Incredible Marketplace
3545	The Answer Is Staring You In The Face
3546	Did I Say The Perfect Storm
3547	Truth Be Exposed

3548	I Recommend You Put Yourself Into This Program
3549	Revenue Producing Activity
3550	Harvest Open Source Collaboration
3551	I Felt Mine Was The Worst
3552	Are You Ready To Rise To A Brand New Day
3553	Every Word Is Important
3554	What's Your Field Intelligence
3555	Here Are Your Free Safelist Submitters
3556	What You Don't Need To Know
3557	Let's Get Back To Value
3558	Cash In On Education
3559	Earn Bonus Points Each Time You...
3560	Why Marketers Don't Want You To Read This
3561	Want A Free $197 Consultation
3562	Are You Waiting Around For A Bailout
3563	The Dark Side Of Being Negative
3564	Want A Free $297 WP Security Update For Free
3565	Paint Your Dreams
3566	Prospecting Task Force
3567	For Those Who Say They Want More But Still Do Nothing
3568	Learn To Market Online
3569	Instant Results
3570	Why You Need To Be Direct And Clear
3571	Sorry I'm Late
3572	Recognizing Superfluous Barriers
3573	Request The Best
3574	Your Private Invitation To The Biggest Sale Of The Year
3575	Zero Marginal Costs
3576	Processing Dot Dot Dot
3577	Persuasive Sabotage Taps Into A Fortune
3578	Fast Friday Fancies
3579	Here Are Some Of The Results
3580	Why An Open Color Works Best
3581	We All Need To Play
3582	But Hey - It's Your Life
3583	Information Is Great But
3584	I've Yet Come Up For Air
3585	You Don't Have To Wait

3586	Do You Know What The Internet Is For
3587	Consider Gel Or Mousse
3588	Gardening Is Therapeutic
3589	Don't Believe Fake Screenshots
3590	Great Systems Succeed
3591	I've Received Emails Begging Access For This
3592	Launching Rockets Of Desire
3593	More Sales For Your Business
3594	Stable Reliable Trustworthy
3595	Call To Action Headlines Snatch Your Reader's Attention
3596	How To Create New Ideas
3597	The Wealth Revolution Is Here
3598	How To Stop Short Of Your Dreams
3599	What You Can Do Now
3600	Don't Put Undo Pressure On Yourself
3601	It's Hip To Be Square
3602	Nothing Stands In Your Way
3603	Have They Traveled The Path You're About To Take
3604	How Long Have You Been A Member
3605	The Color Of Your Money
3606	Ultimate Control Of Your Income Potential
3607	A Few Clicks Of Your Mouse And It's Done
3608	Can You Pass The Secret Test
3609	Want To See Where The Future Is Headed
3610	Related Niches For Cross Promotion
3611	One Little Bit Left
3612	I'm Going To Show You How To Do This
3613	New Products Dominate The Economy
3614	Populate Your Spreadsheet
3615	Click The Order Button
3616	Follow Through With Voice Projection
3617	Research Takes Time And Money
3618	Hitting Psychological Triggers
3619	The Kiss Test
3620	Rare Hidden Traits
3621	Betting On Small Business
3622	Drink From The Fire Hose Of Successful Marketing
3623	Are You On The Endangered List

3624	Our Crazy Marketing Quilt
3625	Are You Heading For The Dark Side
3626	Calling The Networks
3627	Be Aware Of This Shifting Marketplace Niche
3628	Flip It On Its Head
3629	Take A Good Look At This Update
3630	Do The Full Review
3631	Little Biz Big Money
3632	Three Question Evoke Startling Epiphany
3633	I'm Keeping This Offer Valuable And Extremely Limited
3634	Too Much Too Little Just Right
3635	I'll Do It For You
3636	Target Your Market With Laser Precision
3637	The Story Going On In Their Head
3638	Producing Digital Only Versions
3639	No Fancy Sales Talk Here
3640	Discover The Benefits Of Mobile Marketing
3641	The Interpreneur Saves Their Company
3642	Only Buy What You Want
3643	Make Sure You Have A Dreamer In Your Organization
3644	Resale Rights Product Library
3645	Cash Back Fast
3646	Slip Into The Right Mindset
3647	Examples Of Niche Markets You Can Look Into
3648	My Best Product For Free
3649	Repeat What You're Doing And Expand Your Business Efforts
3650	It Disappeared Overnight
3651	Take Your Ranking To The Next Level
3652	Can You Make Me A List Of 10 Creative Ideas
3653	Grow To Be Heard
3654	Acute Pain Isn't Cute
3655	The Single Most Misunderstood Way To Make Money Online
3656	What We Recommend You Consider
3657	We Almost Came To A Brawl When It Happened
3658	Bring Your Gifts Out In The Open
3659	Find New And Rare Things
3660	Separating Theory From Truth
3661	Listen And Observe

3662	Without This I Failed Miserably
3663	Mightier Than The Rejections
3664	Take The EZ Wealth Tour
3665	Tactics That Really Matter To Customers
3666	Schwing Ding
3667	Unless You're Superman You Couldn't Possibly Do It
3668	We Just Change The Access Code
3669	Satisfy Your Needs Now
3670	Come And Get It
3671	Take Advantage Of Your Peak Time
3672	Coin A Phrase That Gets Notice
3673	Her Love Rules The Internet
3674	What's Keeping You Poor
3675	Never Look At It Again
3676	Conduct Thorough Keyword Research Early
3677	Create More Buy Buttons
3678	Leap Over The Corporate Ladder
3679	You Can Be My Wingman Any Time
3680	Just Like You
3681	They Told Me I Shouldn't Do This
3682	Credit Crisis
3683	Taking You Deep Inside
3684	Moving Fast Because You Need To
3685	Think Of Your Headline As An Ad For Your Ad
3686	Screw The Economy This Idea Is Better
3687	Opening The Door For The Coming Year
3688	Physical vs. Emotional Pain
3689	No One Knows What We Do
3690	Welcome Marketers Advertisers And Affiliates
3691	Close Your Eyes And Inhale
3692	Valuable Lessons For Improvement
3693	How Many Chances Do You Need
3694	Customer Appreciation Coupon
3695	Even Blind Squirrels Find Nuts Once In A While
3696	Revolutionize The Digital Download Industry
3697	Reach Hungry Customers And Get Guaranteed Traffic
3698	You'll Need Dry Shorts For This
3699	Be Very Smart Going In

110

3700	Did You Produce A Video
3701	Unlimited Access Available
3702	Why You'll Never Beat Me At Scrabble
3703	Defining A Clearer Vision For Your Success
3704	Yes It's That Easy
3705	What Can I Do That People Can't Live Without
3706	The Biggest Problem Is Processing All The Money
3707	Intelligence Is Dynamic
3708	Tool For Discovery Used In Marketing
3709	In The Spotlight Now
3710	The Creative Class
3711	Three Goals Of A Business
3712	Created By Us Just For You And Your Friends
3713	The Buy Button Is About To Disappear
3714	Really All This And Starting At Just One Green Dollar
3715	I Met Someone Who Changed My Life Forever
3716	Are You A Real Person On Video
3717	Just Pure Salesmanship
3718	Tell Me Something I Don't Know
3719	This Is Way Too Important
3720	Must Have A Specific Offer
3721	Write A Self-Help Book
3722	Stand Out Dynamically From Your Niche
3723	Powerfully Teaching One Thing
3724	How Much Defends Upon You
3725	You'll Understand Why This Is Available Today Only
3726	How Keyword Density Impacts Your Page Rank
3727	My Inbox Is Jammed
3728	Invest In Virtual Real Estate
3729	This Is So Impressive It Will Destroy The Marketing Paradigm
3730	OK It's Your Turn Now
3731	Cloning Your Own Possibilities
3732	Style Guide To Success
3733	Will It Get Worse
3734	Achieve A Different Reality
3735	Getting Your Corner Stones In Place
3736	Frame It From The Advantage
3737	Push On Your Pleasure Centers

3738	You're Being Ripped Off
3739	Huge Thumbs Up
3740	Why Would You Want To Do That
3741	Recession Busting Ideas
3742	Weed Out The Losers
3743	We're Waiting For You
3744	This Course Will Help You To Avoid Failure
3745	Trend Data
3746	We'd Like To Start Placing Customers Under You
3747	Article Marketing Research For Your Niche
3748	Found Myself Questioning Everything
3749	Keep It Authentic And Moving
3750	Here's What Success Means To Me
3751	Sleepy Sunday Secrets
3752	A Knowledge Based Economy
3753	Good News Galore
3754	Writing Headlines Can Be Sticky
3755	Custom Web Programming
3756	Congratulate Yourself For Doing This
3757	Visual Process Maps
3758	Get A Surprise
3759	Show It To Me Right Now
3760	Where Do You Want To Go
3761	Tap Into Thousands
3762	Simple Screenshots
3763	Be Sure There's A Demand
3764	The #1 Wealth Builder
3765	Want The Whole Scoop
3766	The Holy Grail Of Marketing
3767	What I Have Is The Solution
3768	Whack Them On Your iPod
3769	Tell Their Story Not Yours
3770	What Emotion Do You Want To Create
3771	Why I Wanted A Copy
3772	Ciao Bella
3773	101 Tips
3774	Do A Once Over Before Presenting
3775	It's An Immediate Free Download

112

3776	Let Me Share A Little Example
3777	Who Are You
3778	Your Headline Will Make Or Break You
3779	Committed To Results
3780	Only 8 Emails And No More
3781	It's Extremely Important That You Secure Your License Now
3782	Money-Making Internet Business In Steroid Heaven
3783	Want Some Valuable Information
3784	Reward Yourself
3785	Get Your Product Out There Fast
3786	Stand Back And Admire The Answer
3787	Reinforce Their Problem
3788	Is Your Marketing Forecast Stormy
3789	I'm Going To Ride It One More Time
3790	Are Your Emails Being Delivered Opened And Clicked
3791	Honest And Profitable
3792	Don't Try Harder Try Easier
3793	I've Never Liked The Odds
3794	Achieve Your Full Potential
3795	Scientific Advertising
3796	If I Could Just Do This
3797	The Marketing Zombie Apocalypse
3798	Use These Tools To Get A Feel
3799	Infects The Masses
3800	Mobile Solution
3801	License Your Product To Me
3802	Need A Different Perspective
3803	The Answer Is Simple Time Equals Money
3804	Hypnotic Squeeze Pages
3805	Settling For Scraps
3806	I Want Buyers Not Just A List
3807	The Greatest Of All Time
3808	Meeting Your Quota
3809	Needed Cash Injection
3810	This Isn't Some Kind Of Sales Gimmick
3811	My Must-Read List
3812	Grab A Huge Discount Right Now
3813	The Big Light Bulb In My Head

3814	Ultra High Quality
3815	Body Language Moves Your Audience
3816	Thousands Of People Want To Get Their Hands On These
3817	Is Your eCommerce Biz Providing You Significant Growth
3818	The Secret To Building A Massive Financial Success
3819	It's All About The Traffic
3820	How Success Become Self-Perpetuating
3821	Proven Success Lessons
3822	Why It Takes So Long To Create A Product
3823	Your Own Electronic Mail Slave
3824	Crushes Your Competition Into A Thousand Tiny Pieces
3825	Applying New Methods
3826	Don't Lead Yourself Down The Wrong Path
3827	Share Your Results
3828	Hot Ways To Sell Your Products Like Crazy
3829	Earn An Extra 3000 Points Today Only
3830	Cutting Edge Technology Is Available For Beta Testing
3831	Learn 12 Basic Secrets Of A Successful Business
3832	Scrape Up True Grit
3833	You Like Special Deals Don't You
3834	Can You Model That Business
3835	A Professional Blogger's Check List
3836	Join On Online Panel
3837	Don't Wait Too Long
3838	What Dogs Need Is People Training
3839	Simply Attribute Contributing Resources
3840	Gain That Self Confidence You've Desired
3841	The Most Important Part Of Living
3842	Why Follow The Corporate Ladder
3843	Old Time Talk
3844	Listening Is An Art - But Action Is The Answer
3845	Seeking Creative Solutions
3846	Ancient Language
3847	Establishing Page Quality Videos
3848	Conquer Fear Through Knowledge
3849	Things Weren't Looking Good
3850	Easy Reasons For Failure
3851	Why Others Are Eavesdropping

3852	You Got Any More Of Those
3853	Hot New Advertising Program Delivers
3854	Feel Completely Lost And Isolated
3855	Stop Read And Learn
3856	Find And Create Hot Topic Products
3857	Access The Bonus Area
3858	Customers Every Single Day
3859	Your Mail Is Being Sent
3860	If You Didn't Care You Wouldn't Be Here
3861	Get Out Of The Way Of Success
3862	A Marketing Pandemic Will Soon Be Set Free
3863	Big Turn Around Makeovers That Will Change Your Life
3864	Factories No More
3865	When It's Perfectly Wrong
3866	Cash In On New Product Trends
3867	Got A Second To Make A Fortune
3868	Gain Invaluable Insight Into This Unique Opportunity
3869	Not Just More Stuff
3870	Solving The Attrition Problem
3871	Want Traffic Cash
3872	Playing To Win Or Waiting To Fail
3873	Christmas Cash Flow
3874	Can Never Make Enough Eye Contact
3875	Brand New Potential Profit Center
3876	Your Knowledge Give You An Advantage
3877	Supercharge Your Ability To Communicate
3878	Only Wishing You Could
3879	Let Me Explain
3880	Five Places Where You Can Find New Products To Sell
3881	Quiet And Make Your Fears Disappear
3882	Create A Killer OTO
3883	What Other Slants Can Your Find Tweak And Exploit
3884	Create Your Own Automated Income Stream
3885	Amazing Free Offer Will Skyrocket Your Traffic
3886	Lack Of Income Is No Big Deal
3887	Lack Of Content Loses Them
3888	Turn It Into A Monster Product
3889	Be The Envy Of Your Marketing Neighborhood

3890	Hype vs. Exaggeration
3891	Who's Your Favorite Cartoon Character
3892	What An Amazing Lineup
3893	Flying Off The Digital Shelf
3894	Request Your Free Bonuses
3895	Who Is The Most Innovative Person You Know
3896	No More Thuds
3897	Spoon Fed Money Making Ideas
3898	Thanks For Downloading Our Offer
3899	Why Writing Sales Letters Is So Hard
3900	No Skills No Experience No Excuse
3901	Make A Great Gift
3902	Post Unlimited Ads
3903	Free And Paid Channels
3904	These Tools Are Highly Effective
3905	Just Making Sure
3906	Successful Cookie Cutters
3907	Key To Continued Success
3908	I Want To Hear More
3909	Time Spacialization Skills
3910	Promise Of The Future
3911	Still Questioning What To Supply
3912	Keep Your Body Serif Fonts
3913	We're Not Stopping Development
3914	Now You Can And Now You Will
3915	Outstanding System You Must Use
3916	Setting Your Short Term Goals
3917	Can Copy And Content Co-Mingle
3918	Offer These And No One Will Ask For A Refund
3919	There's Too Much Information
3920	A Priceless Experience You'll Never Forget
3921	Become Part Of Something Real
3922	Behind The Scene Search Engine Optimization
3923	Proven Educational Platform
3924	What Kind Of Experience Is Needed
3925	WARNING Your Personal Information Is Being Sold
3926	Future Millionaire
3927	These Prices Will Cause Them To Switch

116

3928	People Do Judge Authors By Their Covers
3929	Fast And Furious Headlines
3930	This Opportunity Is Yours For The Taking
3931	Consider Setting A Physical Reason For Shutting Down An Offer
3932	Are Your Customers Paying Promptly Enough
3933	Your Best Testimonial Is Yours
3934	Giving You More Money
3935	Your Children Get Only One Childhood
3936	Do You Really Want To Struggle Online Year After Year
3937	Select The Right Topic
3938	I Fully Endorse This System
3939	Digital Product Management
3940	No Overhead And Definitely No Pile Of Stuff
3941	What To Creatively Change In Your Life
3942	Why The Right Tools Are So Vital To Your Business
3943	The Naked Truth About Me And You
3944	Provide A Thank You
3945	Breaking News Story
3946	Start Charging More For Your Same Products Or Services
3947	What's Your Current Strength
3948	Unlimited Upload Capacity
3949	Map Out Every Task And Destroy Potential Problems
3950	I Want To Help Them Get That Done
3951	Designed To Earn Monthly Income For Life
3952	A Whole New Mind
3953	[ORDER HERE]
3954	What's Education Really For
3955	Most People Don't Want To Buy This
3956	You Really Should Check It Out
3957	Ads That Stick In Your Mind
3958	Get Awesome Footage
3959	Excess Inventory
3960	Find 10 Different Markets Then Focus On Only One
3961	You'll Want To Chose This Option
3962	Will Truly Amaze You
3963	Times Are Changing Every Nano Second
3964	Create Projects With The Ultimate Advantage
3965	Reach Brand New People

3966	Can You Make It With Search Marketing
3967	That's Not Even The Whole Story
3968	No Prescription Necessary
3969	Now A Devoted Believer
3970	Is Your Money Passing You By
3971	Marketing Knows No Boundaries
3972	A Great Optional Strategy
3973	Actually That's A Lie
3974	Spikes That Come Out Of Nowhere
3975	Telling Lots Of Stories
3976	Resources To Generate More Revenue Online
3977	Win Higher Page Rank
3978	Drown All Your Sorrows
3979	No More Scheduled Meetings
3980	Clean Up Everything Around You
3981	How Can You Tell Which Products Sell
3982	Snap Your Fingers
3983	Change The System Not The Symptom
3984	A Grotesque Understatement
3985	Your Income Will Compound
3986	Take In Information
3987	I Found Your Wallet
3988	Auction Off Your Skills
3989	My Blog Is Cruising
3990	Hands Free Web Page
3991	Sponsor These Great Brands
3992	The Snowball Effect
3993	Moving Forward To Prosperity
3994	Charging High Margins
3995	It's Important How You Phrase Things
3996	It's What You Do Next That Counts
3997	Access The Web From Your Phone
3998	Explore Deep Space Of Internet Marketing
3999	This Back End Logic Makes Things Happen Fast
4000	The Best Possible Way To Start
4001	I Created This Out Of Frustration
4002	Define Your Target Market
4003	Why Can't You Just Tell Me Everything All At Once

118

4004	Rely On Your Trusted Partners
4005	Form Your Own Corporation Without An Attorney
4006	Don't Allow Your Creative Muscles To Atrophy
4007	Receive 100 Ideas Every 7 Days
4008	Name You ME-ME
4009	It's Now Up And Running
4010	Get Higher Clicks And Better Conversions By Joining Today
4011	Here's Our Latest Video
4012	It's Just Too Easy Not To Get Successful Results
4013	The Key Ingredient
4014	That's Pure Bull Skin
4015	We All Do It For The Love Of It
4016	I'll Personally Answer Your Marketing Questions
4017	Laugh Giggle Or Groan
4018	You Think I Might Be An Axe Murderer
4019	Wish You Were Here
4020	Cash Back Reward Based Advertising
4021	Test Drive This One For Yourself
4022	Get Your Hands On My Update
4023	How Foreign Policy Effects You
4024	Fast Track To Earning Money Online
4025	Running An Information Marketing Business
4026	What Is It That You Absolutely Must Have Right Now
4027	Run Down A Complete History
4028	More Than Just The Facts
4029	If We Could Only Have It Done For Us
4030	Without The Technology You'll Never Know
4031	You're The Person To Give It To Them
4032	Strengthen You Core Muscles
4033	Your Unconscious Mind
4034	What's Going On
4035	You're Going To Be Grateful I Taught You This
4036	I Know The Process You're Going Through
4037	Access To Consult Someone In Authority
4038	Position Yourself As An Instructor
4039	Promoting Affiliate Programs Is Only One Business Strategy
4040	My Secret Diary
4041	Stop Editing Your Spoken Thoughts

4042	Brand New Markets
4043	You Get What You Pay For
4044	Different Approach And Solution In One
4045	Young And Foolish
4046	Just Sitting In Front Of Your Computer
4047	Let The Stress Finally Vanish
4048	The Secret Of Making People Like You
4049	Fools Recklessly Believe
4050	What To Do With Your Hands
4051	Avoid The Crap Cluttering The Marketplace
4052	Dance The Night Away While Your Business Grows
4053	As I Share These Truths
4054	For The Past Several Years
4055	You'll Need These Tools To Succeed
4056	The World Judges You
4057	Natural Modern And Creative
4058	Learn How To Protect It
4059	Log Into Your New Account
4060	Selling Your Foreign Language Rights
4061	This Makes Me Sick
4062	Putting Your Website On Audio Autopilot
4063	Get Others To Endorse You
4064	Are You Missing Something
4065	Generate Profits Online
4066	What Skills Should You Have In Producing Teleseminars
4067	All Out War - Are You Ready
4068	The Most Rewarding Things I Do
4069	Narrowing vs. Generating Options
4070	I'm Not Too Embarrassed To Admit It
4071	Where To Go From Here
4072	Accidental vs. Intentional
4073	Up To The Minute Sales Data
4074	Proactive Team Work
4075	Invisible Buy Buttons
4076	Whether Or Not To take Action
4077	Got The Answers
4078	List Building Problems
4079	You Never Dreamt Of This Before

4080	Dance And Stretch
4081	It's A Great Time To Be A Writer
4082	Don't Just Stay Where You Are - Leap The Competition
4083	Mouth To Mouth Promotion
4084	Key Ways To Raising Money The Easy Way
4085	You're Now In The Very Best Company
4086	A Report You've Been Anticipating
4087	Seize The Power
4088	Get Affiliates To Fall In Love With You And All Of Your Offers
4089	Don't Roll Over This Week And Play Dead
4090	Free Emotional Tune-Ups
4091	Secrets That Drive Men Wild
4092	Chat With Our Team
4093	Return To The Resting Position
4094	From A Standing Start
4095	Avoid Mistakes - Aim Your Business In The Right Direction
4096	Home Based Business Is The Wave Of The Future
4097	Relabeling Your Nerves
4098	Secret Bonus Section
4099	Bidding Too Much Or Too Low
4100	Streamline And Portable
4101	Fun Is A Big Core Value
4102	Adding Twice The Value
4103	If You Can Read This You Can Follow This Plan
4104	Never Look Back
4105	Cash In On Digital Trash
4106	This Will Change The Face Of Internet Marketing
4107	The Mortal Headline Sin
4108	Advance Testing Systems That Pull Subscribers In
4109	Why This Is So Irresistible
4110	Enlighten Your Readers
4111	Can't Make This Insane Offer Available Forever
4112	Get In Early
4113	Proud To Be My Own Boss
4114	They Said It Was Easy
4115	Better Results Mean More Profits
4116	Google Has Changed
4117	Raining Cash From The Sky

4118	Here Is Exactly How To Succeed With Safelists
4119	Not Long After The Ink Dries
4120	Forget The Camera
4121	Make An Appointment
4122	Visual Presentation Converting The Best
4123	Traffic Exchanges Take Too Long
4124	Engage Them Into The Next Step
4125	Dancing For Joy
4126	No Email Address Required
4127	Why Pre-Foreclosures Are The Best Profit Opportunity
4128	Giving You The Best Price
4129	Examine Them Carefully
4130	Use The Right Psychological Triggers
4131	Extra Pay Every Weekend
4132	Never Come Up Short Again
4133	$2,750 Per Month Part-Time
4134	How To Build An Empire
4135	Who's Really Reading Your Manuscript
4136	Skip The Frustration
4137	You're Not Invited
4138	That's Not Where They're At
4139	How A Simple Formula Can Become A Laser Beam
4140	Maximize Your Genius
4141	Will Next Year Really Be Different For Your Business
4142	Frustrated Broke And Ready To Quit
4143	Natural Born Leader
4144	Internet Marketing Is In A Constant State Of Flux
4145	Secret Of Perceived Value
4146	How To Protect Your Identity Online
4147	Magnified Future Prosperity
4148	So Easy A Caveman Could Do It
4149	Download And Profit
4150	This Vicious Cycle Can Be Avoided
4151	Remain Completely Anonymous If You Wish
4152	Don't Lose Your Imagination
4153	Start Small And Build Traffic
4154	Interested In Oldies
4155	Here's What's Happening

4156	Give Me Freedom And Independence Every time
4157	Skyrocket Your Delivery Sales
4158	They Aren't Bad Yet
4159	Addicted To Productivity
4160	Making It More Than That
4161	Taking Full Responsibility For Managing My Time
4162	Work Smart Be Clever And Make Money
4163	If You're Broke Then You Need Us
4164	Permanently Dismantling
4165	Rambunctious Newbies
4166	Risk Is Minimal
4167	Wants + Needs Foster Solutions = Sales
4168	The Internet Has Changed Everything
4169	I Just Found This "No Crash" Hosting Solution
4170	Success In A Proven Mentor
4171	Can You Still Fit Into Your Skinny Marketing Jeans
4172	Time vs. Money
4173	An Eye Opening Journey Into The Abyss
4174	Create Life-Long Financial Independence
4175	Extract The Best Material
4176	You Read The Headlines And Nobody Believes It
4177	Offer These As A Bonus
4178	Built In Feed Back Loops
4179	Has History Taught Us This
4180	How Do You View Social Networking
4181	Weird Pricing Competition
4182	Why Has My Life Become So Dependent On Money
4183	Ridiculously Effective
4184	Time To Check Your Style Sheet
4185	Guaranteed Lowest Price
4186	If It's Important You'll Make The Time
4187	Nerves And Nervousness
4188	The Seven Deadly Sins Of Website Copy
4189	Are All Business People Dishonest
4190	Keep Your Hair Off Your Face
4191	Why's That A Difficult Decision
4192	Don't Leave Just Yet
4193	Cracking The Information Monopoly

4194	Get Your Thinking Around Their Wants
4195	Reinforce Your Credibility
4196	Enhance Your Abilities
4197	Competitors Bumping Your Sales
4198	Feel Great In Seconds Not Minutes
4199	It Looks Like It Was Made Just For Me
4200	A Completely Unique Approach To Cashing In
4201	Your Marketing Hope Diamond
4202	Great Places Products and Services
4203	Producing Content
4204	This Is Pure Gold
4205	No Money Down Can Work
4206	Why These Don't Reply On Luck
4207	Even In A Faltering Economy Creative Opportunities Exist
4208	Not A Technical Wizard What Could You Accomplish With One
4209	Your Direct Link To Success Is But A Click Away
4210	Do You Question Your Assumptions
4211	Weight Losing Guide
4212	One Little Bonus I Forgot To Mention
4213	Don't Miss Today's Deadline
4214	Here's How To Boost Business Profits
4215	Moving Monday Magic
4216	Watch The Magic Happen
4217	This Has Its Own Life
4218	Designed With Sales Triggers
4219	Limited Copies So Order Today
4220	A Dozen New Ways To Outlive Your Doctor
4221	Do Your Headlines Suck
4222	Pushy Prospectors
4223	I Don't Like To Work
4224	Affiliate Making Money Systems
4225	The Sweet Spot
4226	So What Is Real Wealth
4227	Can You Top This
4228	Avoiding Information Overload
4229	Why Others Totally Miss This
4230	Still Not Thrilled With Your Website
4231	Trigger Their Emotional Hot Buttons

4270	Learning New Ways To Slice And Dice It
4271	I Love Educating People About This
4272	Guard Dog Hungry And Available
4273	All You Need Is Something That Works
4274	Time To Topple Old Taboos
4275	Words Are What Men Live By
4276	There's Always Something To Write About
4277	How Marketing Could Get You Blacklisted
4278	Gain An Unfair Advantage Over Them
4279	Where To Find The Best Streaming Video Websites
4280	My Job Is To Educate You
4281	Give This Some Serious Thought
4282	You'll Need To Dig Deeper
4283	Get Onboard To Live The Life You Want
4284	My New Year Blowout
4285	Power Of Repeat Sales
4286	I Think On Purpose
4287	Strategies That Create The Highest Long Term Profits
4288	Center Yourself Before Starting
4289	Unprecedented Economic Freedom
4290	Ability And Fortitude
4291	Can Something So Powerful Be So Simple
4292	Earn Revenue From Your Default Ads
4293	Building Ours From Home
4294	Create Viral Cloaked Links
4295	Perfect For Non-Moving Bootays
4296	This Can Never Be Recovered
4297	Then What's The Point
4298	We Handle The Technical Side
4299	Put A Price Tag On And Tell Them
4300	See What You've Been Missing
4301	Satisfy This One Small Desire
4302	You Can't Be In Your Head Here
4303	Get This Free Internet Biz Guide Now
4304	Be Real And Believable
4305	Add Your Own Unique Spin
4306	Immediately Remember Each And Every Word
4307	It Wasn't An Overnight Success

4308	Split Testing System
4309	We All Want To Be Interesting Human Beings
4310	We Close The Cart
4311	If You Love Being In Complete Control
4312	Great Place For Key Point Anchors
4313	Generating Massive Wealth Is A Reality
4314	Listen To Honest Feedback
4315	Let's Have A Marketing Affair
4316	Download Your Free Copy Right Now
4317	Gain The Perspective To Be A Leader
4318	I Absolutely Love Math
4319	Need More Than Just A Little Extra Each Month
4320	Something That's Safe And Easy
4321	We Fixed It
4322	Why Mornings Are More Productive
4323	Why I Still Do What I Do
4324	Rake In Millions Of Dollars Every Year
4325	What 10 Years Online Has Taught Me
4326	Remember These 5 Copywriting Formulas
4327	Now You Can Create Multiple Accounts
4328	Your Double Edge Sword
4329	Identify And Personalize Your Strategies
4330	I'm A Huge Fan Of Virtual Real Estate
4331	Unspoken Tactic That Captures Thousands Of Quality Backlinks
4332	A Name You Can Trust Online And Offline
4333	Do You Really Know Your Customers
4334	High Priced Products That Create A Steady Flow Of Customers
4335	Marketing Sugar Rush
4336	List Building Basics
4337	You Can Have It All
4338	Without Spending A Dime
4339	A Profitable Revenue Sharing System
4340	Hard To Keep Success A Secret
4341	What Are Those Twinkling Lights
4342	Are You Part Of The Inner Circle Yet
4343	Buy One Get One Free
4344	Create Instant PDF
4345	Easy To Use

4346	Big Tip Makes Money
4347	Being Hounded From Every Direction
4348	No More Than 15 Minutes Of Their Attention
4349	Knock Down Dream Blocking Barriers
4350	Leader Wanted
4351	Grab Yours Before This Price Expires
4352	Don't Tuck Your Headlines In The Sand
4353	This Is Not The You Show
4354	Reunion Notification
4355	The Article Beyond Description
4356	Included As A Special Bonus
4357	An Easier Method Of Making Money
4358	Ever Been Accused Of Insanity
4359	Getting It Out There And Marketing It
4360	That's What You Wanted
4361	What Happens When You Ask The Right Questions
4362	Implementation Is More Important Than The Product
4363	Max It Out
4364	Your Final Notice
4365	Make A Fortune Off Of Ignorance
4366	Listen To A Free Sample
4367	I Want To Claim My Spot
4368	It Should Be An Irresistible Offer
4369	The Tradition Continues
4370	Don't Ignore The Power Behind SEO
4371	This Revolutionized The World
4372	Putting 1 And 2 Together
4373	Why Money Doesn't Equal Power
4374	Should Really Get You Excited
4375	Selling Isn't A Dirty Word
4376	How Good Is This Product You Tell Me
4377	Magical Recipe For Making Money Online
4378	Step Into The Moment
4379	Links Above Are Also The Sources.
4380	Final 2 Days
4381	Build Passive Advertising Sources
4382	Watch Your Business Grow
4383	Don't Spend Any More Money

4384	Marketing Kiss Of Death
4385	Every Problem Has Unlimited Solutions
4386	See What You Can Do For Them In Return
4387	Bypass Survival And Failure
4388	Can You Generate Traffic From This
4389	We're Only A Phone Call Away
4390	These Hold The Secrets
4391	Marketing Pleasure Or Pain
4392	Do You Realize Your True Potential Can Change Your Future
4393	Emotionally Powerful Stuff
4394	I Could Tell You All Kinds Of Wonderful True Stories
4395	Product Landing Pages
4396	A Pure Blast Of Creative Genius
4397	Stuff Dragging You Down
4398	Massive Commission Opportunity
4399	Does This Sound Like You
4400	Keyword Generating Sales Not Clicks
4401	Why This Idea Really Works
4402	Don't Settle For Minnow Traffic
4403	Reaching For Words
4404	Silly Holiday Specials
4405	What's The Truth
4406	Why Medium Earth Tone Colors Work Best
4407	It's Your Birthright
4408	Delay May Be Serious
4409	Makes Self-Publishing A Breeze
4410	Miraculous Keys Reveal Unlimited Creativity
4411	Identify Your Magic Zone
4412	Why Their Wallet Becomes Secondary
4413	Blowout Tornado Sale
4414	Representing People's Identities
4415	Garden Flower Blanket
4416	Ad Placements Not Just Anywhere
4417	Instant Turkey Business
4418	Check Out All These Videos
4419	Blown Away By The Whole Prospect
4420	Making Money With A Website
4421	Be A Winner Today

4422	Register While Seats Still Available
4423	Dynamic Copycatting
4424	Whose Fault Is It When Children Disobey
4425	Why People Aren't Having Success Fast Enough
4426	And Why Aren't You Making Money
4427	Yes It Costs Money To Learn
4428	Change Your Life This Year
4429	Wonder Products Still Not Making You Money
4430	Use That Data
4431	How The New Mobile Culture Can Do Business Anywhere
4432	Create Personal Mission Statements
4433	Build Your Own Lists
4434	Punch Your Golden Ticket
4435	The Pivotal Mistake
4436	Energy Flows Where Attention Goes
4437	New Ideas Pop Up Every Day
4438	The One And Only Magic Formula
4439	An Online System You Can Afford
4440	Use Price Increases To Create Scarcity
4441	Wasted Ads
4442	What Kind Are You Going To Make
4443	But Only Men With Imagination Can Take It
4444	We're Getting So Many Inquiries
4445	Advertise With Style Using Timeless Ads
4446	Don't Know What To Say
4447	They Literally Sell Themselves
4448	Self Organizational Learning
4449	This Huge Market Is Growing Fast
4450	5 Fast Ways To Explode Your Opt-In List
4451	Your Video Journal
4452	My Ultimate Money-Making Strategic System
4453	How To Always Turn A Profit
4454	Search Engine Ranking Factors
4455	Brag Some More
4456	Online Coaching Offers Big Educational Opportunities
4457	Is That Really True
4458	Mentally And Psychologically Engage Your List
4459	Business Gets Done In Person

4460	Start A Daily Video Journal
4461	Last Minute Shopping
4462	The Customer Advantage
4463	Wealthy Behavior
4464	Keys To Success
4465	More Money For The Same Work
4466	This Will Make You Feel Powerful
4467	Time Flies When You're Making Money
4468	Secrets For Income Acceleration
4469	Commence Typing
4470	Discover This Tasty Gem
4471	Strategically Add Testimonials
4472	You Can't Make Sales If You Don't Have Customers
4473	You Won't Want To Cancel This Membership Ever
4474	Starting Before You're Ready
4475	Generate Sites Faster Smarter & Cheaper
4476	Your Life Can Change Dramatically
4477	In The Zone
4478	I Make Money Online
4479	How Shall I Fill My Time Now
4480	That's Not An Effective Way To Market
4481	Moral Hazard Heading Your Way
4482	Still Keeps The Money Rolling In
4483	Have You Updated Yet
4484	Walk You Through The Main Overview
4485	Overcome Dismal Results
4486	Lethal Power Of The Hole Punch Method
4487	Did I Finally Get This Idea Through To You
4488	You'll Never Be Left On Your Own Ever Again
4489	Making New Connections
4490	Huge Money Maker
4491	Break It Down Into Easy
4492	Perhaps You Would Love To Own This
4493	Getting Your Business Off The Ground
4494	Here's The Full Range Of Benefits
4495	Be Committed With Your Story
4496	Promoting Value Based Priorities
4497	Your VIP Registration Is Confirmed

131

4498	Put Yourself First
4499	What Are Their Emotional Hot Words Or Buttons
4500	Position Them As Your Students
4501	Rest And Relax
4502	Start Winning Today
4503	So This Is What I'm Going To Do To Help
4504	Go Ahead, Make My Data!
4505	Two Biggest Challenges Beginners Face
4506	Establish Your Pre-Eminence
4507	All It Takes Is A Little Bit Of Elbow Grease
4508	Share The Story
4509	Imagination Is Your Greatest Opportunity
4510	Make Marketing Your Top Priority
4511	It Has Everything To Do With You
4512	You Can Change Your Mind
4513	Think Back To How Life Felt Before This
4514	Catch This Business Opportunity While It's Hot
4515	First Question
4516	Common Ways To Die Quickly Online
4517	The Real Sinister Side Of Failed Continuity
4518	New Trend Brewing
4519	Nice Power And Influence
4520	Overcoming Writer's Block
4521	There's No Other Way To Succeed
4522	Most People Don't Know This
4523	Marketing And Sales Aren't 2nd Class Jobs
4524	Final Words Of Encouragement
4525	Why We're Unique
4526	Failure Is Schooling
4527	Works Like Viagra For Your Campaigns
4528	Play Catch With Cash Anytime
4529	What's Your New Direction
4530	We All Go Through This
4531	How Real Can It Get
4532	Claim Your Role
4533	Advanced Notice
4534	Snafu Disasters
4535	Ask Quality Questions Receive Quality Answers

4536	Smart Marketers Are Taking Notice
4537	The Marketing Effect On Our Environment
4538	Every Crunch Helps
4539	Start Spreading Light
4540	Find Out How Much Real Advertisers Are Paying
4541	Upload Your Future
4542	Time To Quit That Sucky Day Job
4543	Magnetize Your Efforts
4544	Guess Who's Figuring This Out
4545	You Don't Need All Of This Stuff
4546	In The Space Of Just THREE Years
4547	First Contact
4548	The Why What How And What If
4549	The Message Mess
4550	Check Out My Facebook Profile
4551	The Truth Is It's Too Unrealistic
4552	Together We Will Create An Incredible Team Of Experts
4553	Rethink Your Links
4554	Friendly World Class Customer Support
4555	This Solved My Problem
4556	My Misfortune Is Your Luck
4557	Open A Store For Peanuts
4558	They're Always Looking For People Who Get It
4559	Post Holiday Deals
4560	Leave Your Comfort Zone Cocoon
4561	Use My Fulfillment Center
4562	What New Marketers Need To Know About Advertising Effectively
4563	I Bet You Made This Mistake
4564	Random Zig Zag Patterns
4565	Ingenious Prospecting System
4566	See Cash In Days From Now On
4567	Looking For The Best Of The Best
4568	I'll Start Building Your Business Today
4569	Let The Rest Of The World Know
4570	Feel Guilty About Taking This From Me
4571	Break Into Any Niche
4572	Your Final Frontier
4573	Preponderance Of Proof

133

4574	Looking For An Easier Way To Get Started
4575	Shift Of Interest
4576	Don't Eye F... The Camera
4577	The One Last Place
4578	Incredible Storewide Savings
4579	What's In Store For Your Future
4580	Reputation Created Demand
4581	Stop Making Your Boss Rich
4582	Feeling Overwhelmed Perhaps This Is What You Need
4583	Tiny Time Capsule
4584	Have You Ever Been Up This Situation
4585	Don't Be Left Out
4586	The Day's Recap
4587	Pushes You In Just The Right Way
4588	Pay Per Play Video Ads
4589	Stifle Unplugged
4590	What Do You Collectively Know
4591	Keep The Background Simple
4592	What Branding Can Do For You
4593	Change Your Resolution
4594	Engagement Driven Copywriting
4595	Make Money Passively
4596	You Can See What I Mean
4597	It's Paying Off In Green
4598	Selling Has Little To Do With Slick Ads
4599	I Missed You
4600	As Soon As You Click
4601	Inner Circle Programs
4602	Self Improvement Priority
4603	$1,980 With No Selling
4604	Make A To-Do List
4605	There Simply Is No Limit
4606	Mastering Your Body Language
4607	A New Buzz Phrase Is Just Reaching The Internet
4608	Come Back Tomorrow And This Offer May Be Gone
4609	Concerned About Your Finances
4610	Finding The Power Source
4611	Here Is Just Some Of What You Can Do

4612	The Pressure Is Off
4613	The Manifestation Of Social Order
4614	Punishment & Examination Destroys
4615	How To Cut Credit Card Payments In Half
4616	Get Unfrazzled
4617	Buy New Products That Add To Your Life
4618	Watch The People Popping Out Of The Woodwork
4619	She Hates This
4620	Jump Start Your Brain
4621	Let The Soil Be Your Canvas
4622	Converting Faith Into Results
4623	Why Do So Many People Fail
4624	Best Option Is To Compress It
4625	Create More Profits Than An Internet Slot Machine
4626	Are You Always Sending Something Useful
4627	Click And Convert Cash In No Time
4628	Cash Building Strategies
4629	Let's Play More Video Games
4630	Why Success Happens 20X Faster Today
4631	Customers Will Be Telling You Want They Need
4632	The Women With The Midas Touch
4633	How To Get Rich
4634	Learn To Earn
4635	You've Been Flagged
4636	Control Trial Expiration Dates
4637	Capture Their Attention More Than Once
4638	What's Your Perception Of Reality
4639	Is This For Sale In Your Territory
4640	Pick Up Your Empire And Move
4641	Stick With This For One Minute
4642	Commitment + Perseverance + Opportunity = Failure
4643	Where Incentives Work
4644	Customer Acquisition Costs
4645	I'm Going To Beat You No Matter What
4646	Now's Your Chance
4647	Being Natural Convinces More People
4648	You Have The Power To Create Amazing Profits
4649	Smiling Along The Way

135

4650	End Low Project Morale
4651	Ferocious Debate
4652	Make The Assumption
4653	Your Compensation
4654	Affirm You're The Best Marketer In The Universe
4655	Through Them Bizarre And Unusual Questions
4656	Have You Ever Wondered Why Your Computer Runs So Slowly
4657	Piggy Back On This
4658	Perfecting Relationships
4659	Let's See How You Handle This
4660	Stop Buying Expensive Lead Lists Today
4661	Entitlement vs. Enlightenment
4662	Stop The Money Leak
4663	Tricky Timepieces
4664	This Is An Experiment
4665	Powerful Anchor Points Generate Conversions
4666	Never Been Done Before
4667	Most People Are Never Listened To Let Alone Heard
4668	Respect Their Time
4669	It's All About Trade Offs
4670	Never Send A Lifeless Impersonal Message Again
4671	How To Get Started The Right Way
4672	Test Website Fonts
4673	Why Type Of Product Do People Pay The Most For
4674	The Most Expensive Item In The World
4675	Are Powerful Advertising Techniques Merely A Myth
4676	How About A Whole New Approach To Internet Marketing
4677	Is Your Website On Life Support
4678	I'm Not Removing You Just Yet
4679	Break Through Your Financial Freedom Ceiling
4680	Use These Techniques
4681	The Future Internet Weapon
4682	This Company's On Fire
4683	Build Some Buzz Around It
4684	Your Rat Race Escape Plan
4685	Linking Like A Millionaire
4686	Putting Everyone In Earshot Of Your Marketing Campaign
4687	If Network Campaigns Are So Great Why Haven't You Joined

4688	Inexpensive Video Tips Tools And Techniques
4689	Let's Make The Best Possible
4690	Freedom In An Unfree World
4691	Showcase Your Proposed Specialty
4692	A Great Mentor Is Your Career Doctor
4693	My Cash Empire Is Now Exposed
4694	Rapidly Changing Publishing Landscape
4695	Our Job Is To Succeed
4696	Learn More Right Now - Click Here
4697	Your Headline Brings Them In
4698	Did You Know The 4 Learning Styles
4699	How To Quickly Evaluate A Real Business Opportunity
4700	Now That You've Got It - Keep It Going
4701	Excited & Awestruck No Wonder Why
4702	Up Front And Center
4703	Link Away
4704	Written Video Instructions
4705	What Are You Doing
4706	Higher Chance Of Divorce
4707	This Should Be Your Sounding Board
4708	Large Margin Profits
4709	Significant Approach
4710	B Is For Blogging Your Passion
4711	Great Way For Newbies To Start
4712	Smile While You Sleep
4713	People Don't Look At Crappy Headlines
4714	How Fast Do You Want To Make Money
4715	Great Low Prices Where Affiliates Are Welcome
4716	What Does Your Prospect Really Want
4717	Wicked Is The Word
4718	Why Most Niche Ideas Aren't Good
4719	Rebranding To Increase Sales
4720	GPS Your Own Roadmap To Wealth
4721	Tune In Your Marketing Taste Buds
4722	You Can Try It Out For 30 Days For Free
4723	Habits vs. Destiny
4724	Can't Get Rolling
4725	True Motivation

4726	Effective Ways To Reduce Your Business Costs
4727	Little Money Coming In More Going Out
4728	Do It Yourself Marketing On A Budget
4729	Instant Access To Shocking New Videos
4730	Make Money From Online
4731	Customers Like The Same Face
4732	Is Money A Weakness
4733	The One Easiest To Produce
4734	The Power Of Heroism
4735	How To Look Great On Camera
4736	Improve Your Aim
4737	February Commission Payment
4738	Turn Little Splashes Into Humongous Floods
4739	Revoking User Access
4740	Something Special For Everyone
4741	Let Them Do It All
4742	Look Upward To The Camera
4743	Focused Content I Can Trust
4744	Still Relying On Couch Surfing
4745	Category Launches
4746	It Works On Everyone
4747	It Usually Doesn't Work Out That Way
4748	It Doesn't Matter When Your Headline Sucks
4749	Does Your Child Ever Embarrass You
4750	Plan Of Action
4751	Everybody Will Lose Their Job
4752	Easiest Way Toward Marketing Success
4753	Buzz Surrounding A Highly Anticipated Release
4754	Much Easier Than You Think
4755	Which Approach Would You Rather Take
4756	Why Would We Look Forward To Helping You Make Money
4757	Effective Selling Really Is About Getting Anybody To Do Anything
4758	Bucketing Money
4759	Just Real Traffic
4760	The Power Of The Moment
4761	Let Me Tell You A Little About It Right Now
4762	Legitimate Business Opportunity Leads For Free
4763	What's Worse Than A Hiccup

138

4764	The Secret Headline That Always Works
4765	Create Your Own Personal Morning Ritual
4766	Start Laughing All The Way To The Bank
4767	Digital Marketing
4768	Responsible For Tons Of Conversions
4769	Still Trudging Through The Internet Swamp
4770	Get On The Phone And Start Talking To Them Personally
4771	That's Just Crazy To Me
4772	Wet Their Appetite
4773	What The Keys To Your Kingdom
4774	Ever Consider Name Dropping
4775	List At Least 5 Benefits
4776	Activate A Relentless Vision
4777	I Wouldn't Risk It Not Anymore
4778	How To Become Miss Information Or Answerman
4779	It's Also Quite Expensive But
4780	100% Commission On Every Sale
4781	Back To You Lynn
4782	Your Marketing Lookout Tower
4783	Get Your Daily Alert
4784	Posts By Category
4785	Have Fun With This
4786	Shifting Through Available Information
4787	Billions Up For Grabs
4788	We Know We Look Good
4789	Before Moving Forward
4790	Member To Member Payments
4791	Debt Drink And Drugs
4792	Texting In The Shade
4793	Confidence Is A Choice
4794	Write Your Own Paychecks Every Day
4795	The Red Light Challenge
4796	Walking Out On A Horrible Boss
4797	Time To Infuse The Power
4798	Blogging For Dollars
4799	Richard RIVO Interviews
4800	Liberating Financial Freedom
4801	The Scarcity Must Be Real

4802	I Worked Hard For Over 40 Years
4803	Free Overnight Shipping
4804	Go Where The Money Is
4805	How To Earn Money
4806	I've Got The Product If You've Got The Traffic
4807	The Price Stake Out
4808	We Don't Want To Waste A Lot Of Money
4809	Fulfilling Dreams Takes Money
4810	Win Advancement
4811	When The Truth Starts Hurting
4812	7 Social Network Profiles
4813	Site Targeting
4814	Get Mesmerized Visitors
4815	Log Into The Membership Site
4816	It Takes 200 People To Deliver This
4817	This Is Your Watershed Moment
4818	Great Headlines Generate Sales Every Second
4819	Ambition And Achievement
4820	On The Spot
4821	You Think This Is The Best Offer You've Ever Seen
4822	It's Not For Over-Thinkers
4823	Why I Used To Be Broke
4824	Sharing My Strategies From The Stage
4825	Cold Conversions Reheating Up
4826	Cascades Of Cash
4827	Can't Say Thank You Enough
4828	Deliver Quality To Targeted Prospects
4829	No Guess Work Involved
4830	Is Your Consumer Always In Charge
4831	Headlines That Grab A Reader's Attention
4832	All I'm Trying To Do Is Get It Right
4833	Roll With Your Imperfections
4834	Open Your Presents
4835	Tell Your Boss Goodbye
4836	I Hate When People Fail Online
4837	Easiest Business Model On Earth
4838	Experience A Fantastic Conversion Rate
4839	How To Get 'Em Done Fast

4840	Post Your Free Ad Right Now
4841	Fast Simple Budget Friendly
4842	A Wide Range Of Nets
4843	Following Up On The Auto Follow Disaster
4844	Unconscious Signals That Distract
4845	Pretty Good vs. Highly Productive
4846	Get Expert Help
4847	Why They Dream About It
4848	Buckaroos Are Back
4849	Switch It Up
4850	It's Better If It's Not Perfect
4851	Hook Them In
4852	The Mind Has To Answer
4853	It's All About Precise Planning For Financial Success
4854	Testing New Killer Karaoke
4855	You'll Never Be Poor Again
4856	Whiff Of Irony
4857	One Of Earth's Greatest Treasures
4858	The Thinking Brain Likes Power
4859	What's The Difference Between McDonalds And Coca Cola
4860	Prepare For The Affiliate War
4861	Stay Tuned For Complete Details
4862	Acting Decisively
4863	Scared Of New Heights
4864	Google Flags Coming
4865	Stand Up And Demand Success
4866	Discover The Angles
4867	How To Set Up The Ultimate Marketing System
4868	Your Book Can Effectively Change Lives
4869	Don't Stop Now
4870	What I'm Trying To Say
4871	Move On To What Works
4872	St. Nick Pick
4873	You'll Have Full Product Resell Rights
4874	So Don't Delay Secure YOUR Place Today
4875	Watch Your List Start Growing Like Crazy
4876	You Need Their Commitment That They Want It
4877	Solid Colors Tend To Work Best

141

4878	Category Personal
4879	Never Have To Owe Anyone
4880	Here Are Some Video Examples
4881	Save BIG I Mean Huge
4882	Business Home Internet Marketing Opportunity
4883	Most Fall Flat On Their Face
4884	Build Your Own Safelist Starting Right Now
4885	Help Yourself Generate A Full Time Income
4886	Scanners Speed Read
4887	Reap The Benefits
4888	Unused Knowledge Means Nothing
4889	Sleek Sexy Rockets
4890	Decide What To Make
4891	Resume Sites Offer Better Service Results
4892	Why I'm So Thankful
4893	What's The One Thing You Do Best
4894	Want To Sell Your Music CDs
4895	Call Today To Secure Your Seat
4896	Categorically Boost My Response
4897	Once You Sign Up
4898	Learn How To Create A Winning Mindset
4899	Advanced Word Marketing Tactics That Work
4900	Incremental Innovation Markets
4901	Take Your Free Position Right Away
4902	Things Too Costly
4903	Simple Way Google Made Us #1
4904	Building Up Your Skills
4905	No Jumping Through Hoops
4906	Websites Die From Lack Of Sales
4907	Security Is Paramount But Content Is King
4908	Listen To Your Intuition
4909	It's Not My Thing - It's Their Thing
4910	Careful Who You Sit Next To
4911	A Niche Is A Living Breathing Entity
4912	We've Learned Our Lessons The Hard Way So Listen Up
4913	You Need To Hear This
4914	Building A Support System
4915	Turn You Messes Into A Message

4916	Get Paid First
4917	5 Biggest Reasons Why I Should Buy Your Product Or Service
4918	Trust And Inspire Yourself
4919	What Value Do You Provide
4920	Are You Hiding Behind Your Computer
4921	Now You Can Get What You Really Want
4922	Perfecting The Process
4923	This Isn't The Next Fad - It's Here To Stay
4924	Staring At A Blank Monitor
4925	How Badly Did You Always Want This
4926	First Thanks For Purchasing My Course
4927	Where Insecurity And Fears Reside
4928	Generate Immediate Cash With This Product
4929	This Year's Hottest Offer
4930	Are You Sitting Down For This
4931	The Joy Of Collaboration
4932	The Answer Would Be Priceless
4933	What Can You Do That's Different From Your Competition
4934	Here's What Really Happened
4935	Stuff You Already Know How To Do
4936	Get Ultra Focused
4937	Working For Yourself Is Addictive
4938	Lest I Forget
4939	Alternative Approach From Failure To Success
4940	How White And Black Disrupt Video
4941	Cut Out The Marketing Middleman
4942	Today We're All In The Art Business
4943	Updating Your Email Preferences
4944	Disinvent Failure
4945	Being With People You Need
4946	Money Tools To Bank On
4947	Action Generates Reaction
4948	Without Directly Spilling The Milk
4949	Please Don't Hesitate To Call Us
4950	Fall In Love With Your Work
4951	You Can't Put A Price On Truth
4952	Start College Funds For Your Children
4953	Major Core Strategies

143

4954	Grab An Arsenal Of Adrenaline
4955	Keep All The Money You Collect
4956	Getting The Best Possible Results
4957	My Best Marketing Strategy Unveiled
4958	Score Higher With Original Content
4959	Break Solutions Into 3 Action Steps
4960	Send Your Traffic Into Hyperdrive
4961	Highly Paid Marketing Consultant
4962	Avoid The Temptation Of Being Distracted
4963	This Will Change Your Business And Life Forever
4964	Don't Do That - Let It Go
4965	Best Return Of Investment In Marketing Comes From Testing
4966	How Are You Using Your Booster Stations
4967	Eliminate All Possibilities Of Miscommunication
4968	Internal Scoring That Destroys Our Self Confidence
4969	Developing Courage
4970	Budget Friendly
4971	Will You Be Wearing A Mic
4972	What's Coming Across
4973	The Voice In The Back Of Your Head
4974	Learn How To Move
4975	Things Are Getting Serious
4976	People Buy Anything If The Price Is Right
4977	Would You Work For Yourself As An Employer
4978	Outlining All The Key Steps
4979	Search Engine Optimization Is Key To Your Success Online
4980	Make Subheads Bigger In A Different Font
4981	The Shipping Is On Us
4982	Opinions Are Like Lips
4983	Pursuing Market Share Over Profit
4984	I Really Want To Hear About Problems
4985	Think Carefully About Your Decision
4986	Motion vs. Emotion
4987	Soul To Soul Communications
4988	Knocking Down Your Door Wanting
4989	Know The Rules
4990	You Never Know How Strong You Are Until
4991	48-Hour Exclusive Coupon

144

4992	Why 99% Of Programs Are Complete Outright Scams
4993	Working Together We All Win
4994	Skip The Mistakes Most People Make
4995	Why They're Moving In This Direction
4996	Behavioral Marketing
4997	Evaluate Progress And Success Of Your Marketing
4998	Ninja Cash Tactics
4999	Is Anybody Out There
5000	I Await Your Response

Lynn and I hope that this "Think Tank" Series Pro Edition of 5000 Power Phrases will helped you clearly see how to paint your dreams, sell your ideas, and market your messages, propelling each of your ideas and projects toward even more incredible success.

INVITATION - JOIN OUR MARKETING FAMILY

If you would like to join our private VIP mastermind group of professional marketers and receive sample preview copies and updates of upcoming projects and events, simply email us at vip@RIVOinc.com.

We truly wish you the very best and look forward to hearing from you.

Richard & Lynn Voigt
I.M. Education Specialists

145

Concluding Thoughts: 5000 POWER PHRASES Pro Edition

Ever success is built upon a preparing a strong foundation, having a clear vision, and taking positive action each and every day. If you've been searching for a new lifestyle, then you'll find this book directive and inspirational. You can open it to any page and let that page help you rethink possibilities, consider new ideas, open new opportunities, and ultimately experience a more successful and fulfilling lifestyle.

Every problem has a solution! Regardless of your current situation or circumstance, know that you have the power and responsibility to redirect your life in any direction you choose. Simply start thinking about and research the kind of lifestyle that truly appeals to your heart. Begin your new journey by learning everything you can about your chosen subject. When you make that commitment, you'll open more unexpected doors to unique opportunities than imagined.

"Creative Thought Is The Only Reality
Everything Else Is Merely The By-Product Of That Thought."
- Walter Russell

So why not start thinking **BIGGER? It won't cost you any more.** It all starts by never allowing your current life's situation, environment, or so-called friends to limit your path to a happier, healthier, and successful life. After all, whose life is this?

Make a decision to focus on learning something new each and every day. Begin attracting your ideal lifestyle by doing something you love and enjoy. As difficult as it may be, don't allow money to limit your dreams. Focus on the kind of thoughts that make you feel good. Once you learn how to control your focus, you'll have a great chance to see your dreams take shape. You've finally learn to harness the power you always had within, a Universal Energy stream that flows 365/24/7 in any direction your project your thoughts, Good or Bad. Want proof? The thoughts you currently believe and project reflect the life you're currently living. Therefore, if your life isn't happening, change your thoughts, and change your life. It's something only you can hold, visualize, and project, living your dream come true.

Find yourself a mentor and spend more time with people who truly appreciate, support, and foster your dreams. Life may be short, but the thoughts we hold can make our life wider and more fulfilling.

146

About The Authors:

Richard and Lynn develop creative strategies that paint dreams, sell ideas, & market messages   Together, they present a unique team-approach, working side-by-side, helping clients pursue their passions while sharing their skills and diverse expertise as authors, artists, inventors, entrepreneurs, & Internet marketing education specialists.

Teaching by example, they mentor proven self-publishing services, graphic design, video production, domain acquisition, and marketing research of behalf of their company, RIVO Inc – RIVO Marketing, since 1997. They've created & produced hundreds of videos, self-published dozens of books on a wide variety of topics and created thousands of original works of fine art, while refining their Internet Marketing techniques, mentoring programs, and related business website development.

Their mission is to continually uncover new products and services, test new strategies, and network useful solutions with off and online entrepreneurs, small business owners, writers, local artists, models, teachers, students, and marketing professionals.

Their goal is to help clients create an action plan that discovers and connects the missing pieces of the success puzzle. The goals they foster create multiple streams of income for today's volatile economic climate. Their motto is: "Do the work once and allow the work to create additional streams of income for a lifetime."

Feel free to contact them if you have questions or would like to tap into their talents and expertise. They appreciate your feedback and look forward to hearing your success stories.

Contact:
Richard & Lynn Voigt - RIVO
I. M. Education Specialists

RIVO INC - RIVO Marketing
13720 West Keefe Avenue
Brookfield, Wisconsin 53005 – USA
Email Us: support@RIVOinc.com
Website: www.RIVObooks.com
Website: www.RIVOart.com
Website: www.WisconsinGarden.com

CLAIM YOUR <u>FREE RIVO ART PRINT</u> BONUS TODAY

Our RIVO Fine Art Online Gallery currently consists of over **3,000** dynamic digital compositions. As our way of saying **'Thank You'** for purchasing a copy of this book we would like to send you a copy of your favorite **RIVO Fine Art Print**.

To claim your free RIVO Art Print simply:
#1 - Visit **Amazon Books, enter the title of this book** and leave your unbiased review (hopefully positive) or simply send your book review directly to us instead.
#2 - Visit **www.RIVOart.com**
    copy down the DPC # & Title of your favorite work of art
    (example: *DPC 3903 Luscious Calla Lily*).
#3 -Once your review is posted email us at
        support@RIVOinc.com

Please include your name, text copy of your book review, and your favorite RIVO DPC# Art Print Title.

As each request is personally verified, check your email inbox from support@RIVOinc.com for an attachment with your exclusive RIVO Art Print for personal non-commercial usage that you can print or use as a beautiful screensaver. As all Art Prints are under exclusive copyright by RIVO Inc., commercial usage is not permitted without prior written licensing authorization.

Feel free to send us your comments and suggestions, as we would love hearing from you.

RIVO Inc – RIVO Marketing
% Book Review
13720 West Keefe Avenue,
Brookfield, Wisconsin 53005 USA
www.RIVObooks.com

P. S. If you love gardening, come visit our Garden:
www.WisconsinGarden.com

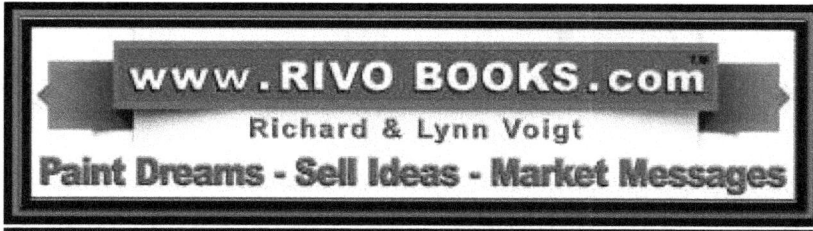

Visit Lynn's Garden: www.WisconsinGarden.com
view hundreds of great garden video blogs Tips

See Richard's Unique Artwork: www.RIVOart.com
view over 3,000 original Fine-Art compositions

Our Book Titles Now Available On Amazon:

THE GOLDEN VAULT OF MOTIVATIONAL QUOTATIONS
Words of Wisdom from The Greatest Minds & Leaders

BABY NAME .ME - 21,400 Names & Nicknames
For Family, Friends, Pets, Natural & Man-Objects

DOODLE DESIGNS Volumes 1-3
For Professionals & Kids Of All Ages
DOODLE DESIGNS – Vol. 1
DOODLE DESIGNS – Vol. 2
DOODLE DESIGNS Coloring Book Vol. 3

Work MORE Accomplish LESS Get FIRED!

ACTION HEADLINES That Drive Emotions – Volumes 1- 6
 Paint Dreams, Sell Ideas & Market Your Message
Action Headlines That Drive Emotions Vol. 1
Action Headlines That Drive Emotions Vol. 2
Action Headlines That Drive Emotions Vol. 3
Action Headlines That Drive Emotions Vol. 4
Action Headlines That Drive Emotions Vol. 5
Action Headlines That Drive Emotions Vol. 6

IDIOMS – IDIOMS - IDIOMS
6,450 Popular Expressions That Put Words In Your Mouth

The CLICHÉ BIBLE - 8,400 Clichés For Sports Fanatics
& Lovers Of Popular Expressions

MORE THAN WORDS
5000+ Marketing Phrases That Sell

HYPNOTIC PHRASING

WARNING-This Book Teaches You How To Grab Eyeballs

YOUR RIGHT TO WEALTH
Becoming Wealthy Isn't Hard When You Know How

WI GARDEN – Let's Get Dirty
Our Wisconsin Garden Guide Promoting Delicious, Healthier Home-Grown Fresh Food, With Tools, Tips, & Ideas That Inspire Gardeners!

MONETIZE YOUR SOCIAL LIFE
Earn Extra Income While Having Fun Online

BABY NAMES
21,400 Unique Baby Names & Nicknames

FUNNY HEADLINES vol. 1
3,500 Outrageous Silly Brain Toots

FUNNY HEADLINES vol. 2
3,500 Outrageous Silly Brain Toots

JOBS
10,240 Career Paths That Can Change Your Life!

MONEY WORDS
Powerful Phrases That Million Dollar Copywriters Use To Make Piles Of Cash On Demand!

GARDEN QUOTATIONS
400 Garden Quotes From The Earth To Your Soul

HEADLINE STARTERS
175,000 Words That Paint Dreams, Sell Ideas, And Market Your Message

BABY NAMES
25,350 Baby Names & Nicknames For Your Family Friends & Pets
  697 pages 7,000 Names with Origin & Meaning plus Top 100 Names, And 2,000 Most Popular Names

CURIOUS WORDS
15,800 Words That Expand Your Mind And Change Your Life

INSPIRING THOUGHTS
That Inspire Happiness, Success & A Clearer Understanding Of Life

MARKETING EYEBALLS
100 Ideas That Can Add Unlimited Subscribers To Your Lists

SECOND OF FIVE
My Early Years- From Birth To High School

POWER PHRASES – Individual Volumes 1 - 10
500 Power Phrases That Trigger Greater Profits

POWER PHRASES Pro Edition – (Complete Series Volumes 1-10)
5000 Power Phrases That Trigger Greater Profits